WRITING FOR ANIMATION

T0316242

WRITING FOR ANIMATION

Laura Beaumont and Paul Larson

BLOOMSBURY ACADEMIC
NEW YORK • LONDON • OXFORD • NEW DELHI • SYDNEY

BLOOMSBURY ACADEMIC
Bloomsbury Publishing Inc
1385 Broadway, New York, NY 10018, USA
50 Bedford Square, London, WC1B 3DP, UK
29 Earlsfort Terrace, Dublin 2, Ireland

BLOOMSBURY, BLOOMSBURY ACADEMIC and the Diana logo are trademarks
of Bloomsbury Publishing Plc

First published in the United States of America 2021

For legal purposes the Acknowledgments on p. xiv constitute an extension
of this copyright page.

Cover design: Namkwan Cho and Eleanor Rose
Cover image © Text supplied by Laura Beaumont and Paul Larson;
additional image © Getty Images

Library of Congress Cataloging-in-Publication Data

Names: Beaumont, Laura, 1956- author. | Larson, Paul, (Screenwriter), author.
Title: Writing for animation / by Laura Beaumont & Paul Larson.
Description: New York: Bloosmbury Academic, 2021. | Includes bibliographical
references and index.
Identifiers: LCCN 2021006785 (print) | LCCN 2021006786 (ebook) |
ISBN 9781501358678 (hardback) | ISBN 9781501358661 (paperback) |
ISBN 9781501358654 (ebook) | ISBN 9781501358647 (pdf)
Subjects: LCSH: Animated films–Authorship. | Animated television
programs–Authorship.
Classification: LCC PN1996 .B386 (print) | LCC PN1996 (ebook) |
DDC 808.2/3–dc23
LC record available at https://lccn.loc.gov/2021006785
LC ebook record available at https://lccn.loc.gov/2021006786

ISBN: HB: 978-1-5013-5867-8
PB: 978-1-5013-5866-1
ePDF: 978-1-5013-5864-7
eBook: 978-1-5013-5865-4

Typeset by Deanta Global Publishing Services, Chennai, India

To find out more about our authors and books visit www.bloomsbury.com and
sign up for our newsletters.

For Bugs…

CONTENTS

FIGURES

PREFACE

For both of us, our first experience of seeing a movie at a theater was Walt Disney's *Dumbo*. These events happened roughly twelve years and five thousand miles apart, but like many people, our first taste of cinematic entertainment was an animated movie. Most of us grow up watching animation. We can all remember our favorite TV cartoons from when we were young. For Laura, it was *The Flintstones* and for Paul it was *Wacky Races* and *Hong Kong Phooey*. It's clear that animation dominates our early years, so it's not surprising that most people have a nostalgia for those shows. Many a conversation at social events ends up with people talking about their favorite childhood animation—sometimes even specific episodes. "The one where Fred and Barney start up their own drive-in restaurant without telling their wives" and "the one where Hong Kong Phooey faces the evil magician." The memories and the joy of reminiscing about them never fails to bind us together with laughter and joy.

We have now been writing animation for so long that we meet people who watched our shows when they were children. Some of them now have children of their own and they too watch our shows. Those same families go to see all the latest animated movies. There are also now a variety of hugely successful animated TV shows for an adult audience, some of which have a massive cult following. Animation is everywhere.

On one level, you could say (and some people do) that it's just "cartoons" but read any book about animators and you will realize how much time, love, and creativity goes into an animation, which is why it can affect us deeply. This is why we love our job. We feel privileged to have a career writing shows and films that people love and remember.

We're not saying it's always been easy. There are very few books or courses aimed specifically at how to write great animation, so we have had to study writing from a variety of forms—including novels, plays, songwriting, comedy, and movies. When we applied the principles we learned to animation, we found that some were helpful, but many were not. So, over the years, through trial and error, we have developed a lot of systems and practices that have helped us.

As our careers developed and we became head writers working with other writers, we found people asking us how we know this "stuff" and whether there is a book they can read. We would have to tell them that no it didn't come from a book, that we worked it out for ourselves. Then came the suggestion that we should write a book. And that's what you have here. This is a manual of all the most valued principles that we use as part of our job in writing for animation, and they actually work, whether you want to write a two-minute short or a feature film.

A new generation of animators, directors, and writers are pouring into the industry and we want to watch the programs and the movies they make. We would like that generation to benefit from our experience, not because they won't do it without help—they will—but because we can save them time. If you absorb the principles in this book, you won't have to go through the same trial and error and the pain of falling flat on your face as many times as we have. We can't wait to see what you create.

FOREWORD

As a producer and creative executive, I spend a great deal of time talking about animation scripts. Much of this discussion is about the demands of animation and live action and how they differ. I've often wished I had a good reference to share on the subject, but it hasn't existed. Until now.

My first job in animation was as the production office receptionist at Warner Bros. Animation. Between greeting guests and answering phones, I typed recording scripts for the Voice-Over department. The task (on a manual typewriter, no less) was to create a dialogue-only version for the actors by eliminating all scene descriptions and stage directions. As a recently graduated theater and film student, I was unaccustomed to reading elaborate, specific descriptions of blocking and physical comedy. In contrast to playwrights and screenwriters, the animation writers were unencumbered by the constraints of time, space, and physics. Their imaginations ran free. They could conjure anything and everything and did so with sensational comedic chops. I fell in love with the medium. I was young and inexperienced enough to be confident I could simply dive in and write for animation, too. These were cartoons—kids' stuff—how hard could it be?

I still have the pages of ideas I submitted to a story editor who was willing to indulge me. More importantly, I have the notes he generously returned to me. While constructive, supportive, and encouraging, they basically translate to, "Don't call us, we'll call you." Turns out playful, precise, character-driven animated comedy is not as easy as it looks. How did the writers make it seem so effortless? I resolved to read every book in print about animation writing and, like Wile E. Coyote, I hit a wall. I couldn't find a single book on the subject. Plan B was to pester the writers with questions, read more scripts, and watch even more animation. That education evolved into my career. Lucky me.

The volume and variety of animation has exploded since then. Technology transforms the medium almost daily. Publishers have kept pace, and there are now many titles covering animation art, production, even how to develop animation-specific ideas. However, books dedicated to the nuts-and-bolts process of animation writing remain scarce. Explaining it may be as elusive as doing it well. All of which adds up to *Writing for Animation* being a rare book. It is an invaluable resource for writers wrestling with the not-at-all effortless task of creating effortless scripts. It's exactly the book I was looking for all those years ago.

Beyond the scarcity of books of its kind, this one is also rare because animation writers of Laura Beaumont and Paul Larson's caliber are few. They are among the most talented and prolific in the field. Working with them is a joy. Their scripts reflect their skill and passion, as does their book. Like master magicians revealing the secrets behind mystifying illusions, Paul and Laura draw back the curtain to offer a virtuosic instruction manual. Lucky you. Lucky us.

By Christopher Keenan,
Producer, Executive, and sometimes Writer.
(Credits include *Barbie, Scooby-Doo, Masters of the Universe, Tom and Jerry,* and *Thomas and Friends.*)

ACKNOWLEDGMENTS

Everyone that you work with contributes to your writing journey, and, as such, all have contributed to this book in some way. Some people do however stand out as particularly significant and therefore we would like to thank the following:

Katie Gallof, for agreeing to read our book proposal and for her support throughout the writing process; Tim Bain, for suggesting we write the book in the first place; Jocelyn Stevenson, for giving us each our big break all those years ago; and Christopher Keenan, for his incredible support and for writing the foreword.

Other significant contributors include Erin Duffy, Adam Long, Marion Edwards, Lisa Pacheco, Marc Seal, Simon Spencer, Rosie Bones, Anna Starkey, Tim Compton, Christine Ponzevera, Alex Jennings, Ian McCue, Abi Grant, Dominic Minghella, Deirdre Kelly, Gail Renard, Jen Upton, Madeleine Warburg, Peter Corey, Ross Hastings, Sophie Finston, Pete Coogan, Andy Defty, Miranda Larson, Conrad Williams, the legendary Sam Barlow, Gary Andrews, Ken Faier, Jamie Anderson, Theresa Plummer-Andrews, Jackie Edwards, Chris Rose, Joan Lofts, Vanessa Hill, Katrina Tanzer, Karen Doyle, Simon Nicholson, James Mason, Phil Gomm, Dave Ingham, Jan Page, Mellie Buse, Hilary Baverstock, Jackie Cockle, Sue Nott, and Tony Collingwood.

Chapter 1

WHY ANIMATION?

A lot of writers will tell you that you cannot learn to write; it is a gift you either have or you don't. There is a small element of truth in that; some writers have more natural ability than others but everyone can get better. Everyone can learn principles of structure and dialogue, and they can learn to apply elements of drama and comedy that will make their stories better. That's what we aim to do here, but before we get into the nuts and bolts of how to make your scripts great, we need to have a reality check.

The Business of Animation

Animation is expensive. It doesn't need to be; it is now possible to create animations on your phone using paper cutouts for next to nothing, but animation as you would see it on TV or at the movie theater is costly to make. At the time of writing, the cheapest form of computer-generated imagery (CGI) animation costs around $15,000 a minute to make. A good one can cost upward of $50,000 a minute. To get a rough idea of a series budget, let's take the lower number of $15,000 per minute. If it's a ten-minute episode, the body of the episode will be around nine-minutes long, giving us a cost of $135,000 per episode. If you're making a series of twenty-six episodes, you then need to multiply that number by twenty-six. That's a lot of money. Your idea for that quirky new cartoon series about a robotic samurai is in fact a multimillion-dollar business proposal.

To illustrate further, moving out of the world of animation for a moment, we are going to look at a show called *Shark Tank* (*Dragon's Den* in some territories). In this show, members of the public are given the opportunity to pitch business ideas to successful entrepreneurs, or "Sharks," in the hope of finding an investor. There are a lot of bad ideas on the show, but there are quite a few ideas that seem like good ones too. But when you watch it, it's amazing how often the ideas that seem good suddenly start to fall apart under the scrutiny of the "Sharks." The idea might be innovative but the numbers don't add up; it might be the best-tasting jelly that's ever been invented but the branding is all wrong. Sometimes the person making their pitch has done everything right, that is, the accounts add up and the marketing plan is perfect, but it turns out that someone has already started something just like it and is six months ahead. The list of the ways that these business ideas can fall apart seems endless. These top entrepreneurs know what they're looking for and know how many different ways a business can fail. But how does this apply to you as a writer of animation?

Most companies that make animated shows either have a lot of money or know investors that have a lot of money. People and companies with lots of money don't tend to keep lots of money if they take too many risks. Now, what if we told you that the way to see your ideas and stories come to life on the screen is as simple as making people feel more comfortable about the risk they are taking? The more comfortable you make people feel, the more stories you'll get to write. And that's what this book is about. That doesn't mean this is a checklist on how to project the right body language and say the right buzzwords. This is about bullet proofing your ideas. It's about the fundamentals of what you need to do to give the industry (and your audience) what they want, at the same time as allowing yourself to be creative.

But, how do you make the decision-makers feel comfortable about choosing your project?

Master the Craft of Writing

Writing animation requires a complex and unique set of skills. To start with, you need to be able to think visually and process your ideas into a series of shots, you need to write dialogue that is both energetic and true to character, and you need to be able to think in terms of dramatic structure. In short, you need to be both technical and creative and, depending on your chosen genre, you may need to be funny too. This may sound daunting, but the truth is that no one is great at all of those things (if they were, *Toy Story* wouldn't have four writers on the credits), but we can all improve our weak areas and get even stronger at our strong ones.

But how do you master the craft of writing? Well, we're going to give you lots of tools that will help you. These tools will make your stories better, and the more tools you master using, the more accomplished you will become as a writer.

Tools Not Rules

There are no rules in writing. Although some people will tell you that there are. Some will tell you that they know the golden rule that you must stick to, the one thing that you must always do when writing a script. This simply is not true. For every rule that someone comes up with, you can find a successful story that breaks that rule. So, we've come up with a toolbox rather than a rulebook. Now, it's important to remember that some tools are more helpful and should be used more often than others. If you're a cabinetmaker, you probably use a saw on pretty much every job you do, but you might use needle-nosed pliers only occasionally. So, we'll be recommending that you use some of these tools in pretty much every story, while others you might only use if you feel like your story is "lacking in something."

It is important to note here that while there are no rules in writing, most shows do have their own format that make them successful—we'll be covering that in Chapter 20. These formats are the "rules" for those shows, but there is no one set of rules that apply to all stories or shows.

Why Animation?

In theory, you could make any TV show as an animated series if you wanted to. But then why are *Breaking Bad* and *Friends* live action? And why were *Tom and Jerry* and *Bugs Bunny* animated? The answers might seem obvious, but we need to break this down to the fundamentals so that your stories always have a strong foundation. Laura once sat in a meeting where a creative with a series idea was pitching his concept to a producer. Part of the conversation went something like this.

                    PRODUCER
        I love the show idea, but why is
        it animated?

                    CREATIVE
        Because it's for kids.

```
                    PRODUCER
        No, I mean why would you animate
        this show? It would work just as
        well if it was live action. Kids
        watch live action too.

                    CREATIVE
        I just think it should be
        animated.

                    PRODUCER
        Ummm . . . Let me put it this way . . .
        This isn't an animated show.

                    CREATIVE
        It is, I've drawn the
        Characters . . .
```

This went on for some time, but hopefully you get the picture. Just to be clear—that show didn't get made. But also to be clear, the person with the idea didn't understand why that show shouldn't be animated and neither did Laura. We had to make quite a few mistakes of our own before our point of view switched from "that producer is wrong" to "I get it, I know the changes we need to make if it's going to be animated." So, it's time to open our toolbox and start tinkering about with the nuts and bolts of animation.

There are three main reasons why a TV show should be animated. These are not in order of priority, and the reason can be any one or a combination of all three.

Fantasy

Let's start with *Tom and Jerry*. Imagine you're Hanna and Barbera and you've just come up with this idea. There's a cat that's trying to catch a mouse and the mouse is always one step ahead of him. You've got great ideas for slapstick comedy and exciting action sequences and you can't wait to get started. So, why are you going to make it animation? Is it possible to do a live action version of the show?

You could get an animal training school to train some cats and mice and then film it with a real cat and mouse. The best we can say about that idea is "good luck with that!" Or maybe, you could get two actors who are good at physical comedy, put one in a cat costume and one in a mouse costume, build some giant props, and you're away. But would that look as good as the Hanna Barbera animation? We doubt it. What if we make it that the characters are not a cat and a mouse but two people who don't like each other? Someone who is big and aggressive chasing around someone who is small, smart, and agile. Well, that might work, but you would lose all the incredible sequences that rely on the cat and mouse scale. If you disagree, just watch the pool table sequence in *Cue Ball Cat*. On top of that, you'd also lose the legacy of cat and mouse conflict, you don't need to explain why Tom and Jerry hate each other; we already know that cats and mice don't get along.

We put it to you that in the case of *Tom and Jerry* the fantasy of two animal adversaries with some cat and mouse traits and some human traits was best realized as an animation series. The fact that everything was a sequence of drawn pictures allowed the freedom to create scenes that would be difficult to recreate in the real world.

There are a number of ways in which fantasy makes animation your best choice of medium. We've just talked about one but the possibilities are endless. Think about *Bugs Bunny*, *Adventure Time*, and *Frozen*. Why are each of those animated? And once you've thought about those, we want you to think a little harder. We want you to really get this stuff and take it on board, and the best way to do that is to think about it, ponder, explore, and get stuck in.

Thinky Time #1

We tried to come up with a scholarly name for these exercises, but hey, you're going to be an animation writer, you have to get used to "silly."

You're now going to come up with some ideas for your very own animated TV show. Yes, you're in the first chapter, and you are already going to create your own show idea. We're going to do this by taking a live-action TV series and giving it a fantasy twist. Think about *The Flintstones*; it's like a family sitcom in a caveman world. *Top Cat* is *The Phil Silvers Show* with alley cats. What about *Scooby-Doo, Where Are You!*? A mystery horror comedy with a talking dog. Now, what if you took *Downton Abbey* and made all the characters mice? What would happen if you set *Blue Bloods* in a beehive?

Now try some yourself. You're going to start by making two lists. First, on the left side of your piece of paper, write down some TV shows. Then, on the right side, write down some ways you could give it a fantasy twist. We'll give you four of each to kick things off, but try and come up with at least ten.

Schitt's Creek	in Santa's Workshop
The Mandalorian	in Medieval Times
The X Factor	in a Vegetable Patch
Shameless	in an Aquarium

When you have completed your lists, it's time to mix and match. Try putting different combinations of right and left together. What would *The X Factor* in medieval times look like? Just run through them in your head and see if any two that you put together make you laugh or excited. This may sound very simplistic, but you'd be surprised by how many times this kicks off a good idea. And it also works with movies. Have you ever seen *Chicken Run*? It's like *The Great Escape* set in a chicken coop. *Oliver and Company* is *Oliver Twist* with dogs.

Some of the ideas this exercise generates might not be great, you might also realize that the idea that you've come up with already exists. That doesn't matter. The whole point is to start thinking about what makes good animation. But, you might have hit on an idea that you really like, and if you have, we don't want you to waste it. Write it down and keep it somewhere; you might decide to develop it later.

Next, we're going to go on to talk about fantasy's not-so-distant cousin.

Hyper-reality

Hyper-reality is a little like fantasy, but for the purposes of understanding animation we need to make a distinction between the two. Fantasy would be a TV series about a talking sponge who lives in a pineapple; it has no basis in reality. Hyper-reality is when that talking sponge can cook 100 crab patties in just a few seconds. Take Scooby-Doo. A talking dog is fantasy, but squeezing a five-foot-high sandwich into one mouthful is hyper-reality. It's kind of real, but hyper.

Fantasy and hyper-reality often exist side by side; many fantasy shows also have hyper-reality in them, but they don't always. Take *Dinotrux*. If you've never seen it, take a moment and watch an episode. *Dinotrux* is packed full of fantasy; all the machines have personalities and can talk. This has no basis in reality. The rest of the show is grounded in a very real world. There are no extreme sound effects and no eyes popping out on stalks; the mechanics of the *Dinotrux* world is for the most part based on reality.

Let's talk about *The Simpsons*. When Mr. Burns built a device that blocked out the sun, that was fantasy. But when Homer fell off a cliff and hit every rock on the way down, it didn't kill him, it just really hurt—that's hyper-reality. Have you ever seen the episode where Sideshow Bob stands on rake after rake, each one springing up and hitting him in the face? That is definitely hyper-reality. How do we know that? When Paul was a kid, he'd seen cartoon characters stepping on rakes quite a few times and wondered if they did spring up like they did on TV. Then one day he was playing in the garden and there was a rake on the ground, so he decided to test it. Just gently in case it really did hurt. It turns out, that it's quite difficult to do gently and it does hurt. Seriously, don't try that one at home. We know that there is no way Sideshow Bob would still be standing after stepping on that many rakes in a row. The action of standing on the rake is real, the fact that it flies up and hits him in the face is real, but the fact that Sideshow Bob goes on to do it about seventeen more times and it doesn't crack his skull, that's hyper-reality.

You may have noticed that a lot of this hyper-reality is very visual. That is a key point. Animation is a very visual medium and perhaps is more related to the movies of Buster Keaton and Charlie Chaplin than it is to many modern TV programs that have more dialogue. Don't get us wrong, animation has great dialogue—the silent era finished a long time ago—but visual humor is a big part of animation and hyper-reality.

Thinky Time #2

Okay, so now you're going to watch some TV. One of the great things about this job is that you get to watch cartoons and it counts as actual work. So, choose an episode of an animated TV series. You can do this with a movie too, but an episode is quicker. Now as you watch it, we want you to think about the hyper-reality used in the animation you are watching. Which parts are fantasy and which parts are hyper-reality? How extreme are the levels of hyper-reality? Different shows will have more or less, depending on the style of the show.

Sometimes the line between hyper-reality and fantasy is blurred, so you may not be able to put everything into a clear category. That's okay. We just want you to think about why stories should be animated instead of live action.

Now this exercise won't give you an idea for a whole show or movie like the last one, but this is more useful than it first appears. Being able to analyze the style of a show is very important, and we'll be talking more about that in Chapter 20. But just so you know, we promise that we won't give you any exercises to do that aren't really helpful—so they're all worth doing! And hopefully they're quite fun too.

Money

You may have noticed a slight flaw in our logic in the last two sections. You can film fantasy and hyper-reality without using animation. So now we're going to look at the exceptions to the rule. Let's go back to *The Flintstones*. That has been made into a live-action movie. What about *Home Alone*? That movie is jam packed with hyper-real animation-type moments, and it's not animated. But there is an element that comes into play with all movies and TV shows, and animation is not exempt. And that's money.

We've already told you that animation is expensive to make, so let's have a look at one particular show to illustrate how budget can influence a decision to animate a show.

Have you seen *Futurama*? You could make that show in live action if you had a huge budget and you really wanted to, but what are the practicalities? Models of futuristic cityscapes can be constructed, giant spaceship sets can be built on huge stages, aliens and mutants can be achieved with prosthetic makeup, and slapstick action scenes can be performed by stuntmen. You also have to make twenty-six half-hour episodes in a year. That's a lot. And it's just cheaper, and often quicker, to draw the images and move them about inside a computer.

You don't need to know the complexities of budgeting an animated series or movie; we're writers not production accountants. It just helps if you're aware of it. What we don't want is for you to put your heart and soul into an idea, then when you get to pitch it to a producer they say those words, "this isn't an animated show." We want you to be more professional than that—and you already are. But just to hammer the point home, do the following exercise.

Thinky Time #3

Remember that episode you watched for Thinky Time #2? We want you to think about these questions:

1. Which scenes would be really tricky to film in live action? If you were a director and you had to film those scenes, how would you do them?

2. How big would some of the sets have to be if it was a live-action show?
3. And finally, does it just look better animated?

A Brief Word about Visual Style

A thought that might be crossing your mind, and that we haven't covered yet, is, what about visual style? Surely just how great it looks is a good reason to animate something? And our response to that is, absolutely yes! Ultimately, some things will just look better in animation. Sometimes it's not about money or logic, it's about creativity. It's about just how gorgeous it looks. Some animations are animated, not because of the financial reasons, but because of their aesthetic. Both *Persepolis* and *Ethel & Ernest* could have been filmed as live action, but you would have lost the unique vision of the artists who created them.

That very same unique vision is what makes animation so diverse. It allows us to produce something as sweet and endearing as *Peppa Pig* (Figure 1) to something as subversive as *BoJack Horseman* (Figure 2). You can make something that looks as simple as *Adventure Time* (Figure 3) or as rich and complex as *The Triplets of Belleville* (Figure 4). There is nothing like animation to whisk you into a world of fantasy and wonder. Sometimes animation is just the best.

Figure 1 *Peppa Pig*, "The Quarrel", June 7, 2007.

Figure 2 *BoJack Horseman*, "The BoJack Horseman Story, Chapter One", August 22, 2014.

Figure 3 *Adventure Time*, "Slumber Party Panic", April 5, 2010.

Figure 4 *The Triplets of Belleville*, August 29, 2003.

How to Get the Most Out of This Book

If you're going to write (or work in) the animation industry, you're going to need to watch a lot of animation. You will need to keep up to date with the latest releases, partly so you know what the current trends are, both in style and in content. If you want to work in animated comedy, you will need to know about *Family Guy*, *Rick and Morty*, and *Bob's Burgers*, but if you're more interested in features you will need to keep up to date with the production slate of DreamWorks, Disney/Pixar, Studio Ghibli, Laika, and Sony.

Another reason for absorbing as much animation as possible is so that you can see how technology is developing. When we first started working in CGI, we had to avoid stories that involved characters interacting directly with water because it was so difficult to animate, but now technology has moved on and it has become easier. It would have been much harder to get the greenlight for a movie like *Moana* (Figure 5) in 2006 than it was in 2016. Similarly, in the movie *Sing*, we see the theater being destroyed by a flood (Figure 6). We suspect that ten years before this, budget and animation difficulties would have meant that the writers would have been forced to come up with a different way to destroy the theater. At the time of writing, crowd scenes are time consuming (and therefore expensive) to animate (especially in CGI and stop-motion) so need to be kept to a minimum. If you

Figure 5 *Moana*, November 14, 2016.

Figure 6 *Sing*, December 3, 2016.

are working on a high-budget blockbuster, then the production will probably accommodate this. But scenes like we see at the end of *Hotel Transylvania 2* (Figure 7) need to be kept to a minimum. It would seem though, that it is just a question of time before developments in software make this cheaper and easier to create.

Figure 7 *Hotel Transylvania 2*, September 25, 2015.

Throughout this book we will be using lots of examples from animated TV series and movies. There is so much animation out there, it will be impossible to keep up with everything, and chances are we will be using some examples of projects you have might not have heard of. That's okay. Where necessary we will provide you with all the information you need to understand the examples when you get to them. In some cases, you might want to run an internet search so that you know a bit more about the project and in others you might want to watch the whole thing. There are also a few movies that will be helpful to watch as you are reading; this will depend on the chapters you are finding most helpful, but in particular we would recommend *Zootopia* and *Shrek*.

You will notice that a lot of examples we use are from animated features. That doesn't mean that this book is just for those who want to write an animated feature—although it does fulfill that role. We use those examples for three reasons:

1. These features are familiar to a lot of people and are easy to access if you want to watch them.
2. Many of the principles used in writing an animated feature are the same in TV and even in a two-minute independent short, so most can be applied to whatever form of animated storytelling you are interested in.
3. Writers of successful animated features tend to be the very best at what they do, so they make great examples.

Bonus Material

Throughout the book, there are various sections titled "Bonus Material." They appear in the same format as this insert, and they contain advice that we feel needs special emphasis.

Brilliant! We've made a great start and you're on your way to being a top-class animation writer. Now it's time to get stuck in with one of the most powerful tools at your disposal.

Chapter 2

GOALS

This is a short chapter. But the information here comes up again in other parts of the book, so it's important to understand.

Goals drive stories. Great goals make great stories. Whether it's Macbeth aiming to be king or Doc McStuffins trying to fix a teddy bear. It is hard to write a story without characters having goals. There have been great movies that are not entirely goal driven, the recent *Joker* movie being a perfect example, but it is hard to think of a successful animation that does not use goals to drive the story. But what are goals and how do we use them most effectively?

To answer that, we want to take you into a different world for a moment. The world of motivational speaking and positive thinking seminars. There are all kinds of seminars you can go on; they usually have words like "excellence" or "power" in the title. They often take place in big hotels or conference centers and have whiteboards and PowerPoint presentations. A rock song might play as the speaker struts out and tells you how to improve your life. We know about these because in a former life Paul went to most of them. Now, there is one thing that most of these courses have in common—they talk about goals. And the goals that you give your characters will work in a very similar way to the goals that you learn at these seminars. You can learn a lot about goals by going on one of these courses, fortunately you don't have to. We're going to tell you all the bits you need to know for your script right here.

First, let's go back to the motivational seminar for a moment. Often the kind of goal these courses promote is how to earn a certain amount of money, say a million dollars, or to land the job as the chief executive officer (CEO) in a big company. Maybe it could be to sell a certain number of phone contracts. These could all work as the character's goal in an animated movie. Usually those goals are a little more off the wall than that, but just to highlight the point, a story about a honeybee who is trying to usurp the Queen and be the CEO of the hive might make a great movie. We will come back later to the reasons why that might work, after we've talked about the fundamentals of goals in storytelling.

There are three things that make a goal work in a story, and we're going to examine them one at a time.

1 Goals Require Desire and Action

A goal is something that a character wants. Whether it's Charlie Brown trying to get the Little Red-Haired Girl to notice him or Elastigirl trying to save the world, these are things that the character wants. But they don't just want them, they set out to get them. A goal with no action or pursuit by the character is just a thought, and a thought on its own does not give us a story. What would happen in the movie if Marlin didn't set off to find Nemo? We suspect that a movie about a fish that was depressed about the loss of his son and did nothing to rectify the situation would have flopped at the box office.

Your character has to want the goal badly enough to spring into action. The more your character wants to achieve the goal, the better your story will be. It's almost like a law of storytelling:

The greater your character's desire, the more dramatic your story will be if it's a drama
or the funnier your story will be if it's a comedy.

If your character just wants to be a king a little bit, that's kind of interesting, but look at Simba in *The Lion King*. Scar killed his dad, took his kingdom, and is now destroying it, Simba *desperately* wants to rule the pride and make things right again. One of the best examples of strong desire comes in the movie *Moana*. The central character, Moana, has the goal of returning the "heart" to Te Fiti. Moana knows this will be a perilous quest, so why does she set out to achieve this goal? First, there is a coconut blight on her island, then the fishermen can't find any fish, then she discovers that there is a "darkness" that is draining the life from the island, and then she discovers that the ocean has chosen her for this quest. This might seem like a lot of good reasons to achieve this goal, but she is still resistant. But then, you have her grandmother's dying words when she tells Moana "you must." Now, there are enough reasons for her to go and, as an audience, we really want her to achieve her goal.

2 *Goals Are Specific*

There is more to a good goal than it just being something a character wants. A good goal also has to be specific. Marlin doesn't want to find just any young fish; he wants to find Nemo. Simba doesn't want to be ruler of any bunch of lions, he wants to take his place as the ruler of the Pride Lands. When you write, the more specific you become, the better your story gets. So, make your characters' goals specific.

Now we're going to drill down into this a bit more. A good way to make a goal specific is to make it "tickable." Now "tickable" isn't a real word (at least it's not in the dictionary at time of writing), what we mean is that if your character were to write his goal down on a piece of paper, he would know when he could tick it off as achieved. Stick with us on this one, because getting this right can mean the difference between a great script and one that is constantly rewritten because it doesn't quite work.

Let's go back to the motivational seminar again. The person doing the presentation has got everyone to write down their goals. Invariably, a few people will have put down something like "to be happy" as their top goal. Which sounds great, but it's not specific enough. Most motivational coaches will tell you that you need to be more specific than that. Chasing happiness is a very vague activity and can send people to the Himalayas in search of themselves. What is it that's going to make you happy? Is it a Ferrari? A million dollars? To be a real live boy? You can't tick "being happy"; it's a state of mind that comes and goes. Your character might end up living happily ever after, but what was the "tickable" goal that led to that moment?

In *Toy Story*, Woody wants to be Andy's favorite toy, but then Buzz turns up and seems to ruin that for him. We could state that Woody's goal is to be Andy's favorite toy, it's something he wants, and it's kind of specific. But how would Woody know he could tick that off on his piece of paper? Like happiness, it is a transient thing. It can change. Andy could state at the end that "you're my favorite toy ever" and then maybe he could tick it off, but what if Andy's mum gets him the latest X-Box for Christmas? Woody might be erasing that tick.

So how do we make it more specific? We make it physical. Something concrete that everyone can see. Animation is a visual medium, and being able to see the goal achieved, something tangible, makes the story stronger. In *Toy Story*, Woody's tickable goal is to get Buzz back to Andy after they get left at the gas station. That is specific and tickable, and we can see when that has happened. In *Beauty and the Beast*, the Beast doesn't just want to learn to love another and earn their love in return.

No, he wants to do it so he can become human again and we see that happen. Great, I'm a human; I can tick that box now. And then he does live happily ever after.

3 Goals Have a Time Frame

Meanwhile, back at the motivational seminar, the course leader has finally got everyone to cross out "be happy" from their goals list and come up with something more specific. He's made them think of a ton of reasons to achieve their goal so now they really want it. The next thing we need is to give that goal a time frame. There's a big difference between earning a million dollars over the course of a lifetime and earning a million dollars in the next year. So, we put a date on achieving our goals. The Beast doesn't just need to earn the love of another, he has to do it before his twenty-first birthday. In *Cars*, Lightning McQueen is desperate to escape Radiator Springs and get to California, but it has to be in time for the Piston Cup tie-breaker race.

In a story, we don't always know the time frame from the beginning, but the better stories introduce one at some point. This is often called the "ticking clock" or a "time lock." Sometimes the time frame changes throughout the story—usually getting shorter to increase the tension.

Goals in Summary

So, we know that our character must deeply desire their goal. It has to be specific, physical, and tickable. It's also better if it has a deadline. Now, let's go back to the idea that we talked about earlier in this chapter again: the honeybee who wants to usurp the Queen and become the CEO of the beehive. That's an idea that is less than one line long, but it just seems to work. Why? Because that one line tells us something very specific that our character wants and we can picture what that would look like when they achieve it. That picture will be different for each person as we don't have all the story details yet, but most of us will imagine something. That is the power of a goal in storytelling.

Thinky Time #4

We know specifically what our honeybee wants to achieve, but now we want you to think more about the other aspects of the goal. Why does he want to become the CEO of the hive? Is he selfish and wants to control the honey supply in the area? Does he think it will be an easy life? Is the Queen evil and oppressing the other honeybees? And what is the time frame? Why does the goal have to be achieved by a set time?

1) Write down five reasons that our honeybee might want to achieve this goal.
2) Write down five reasons for the goal to be achieved within a particular time frame.
3) Decide which combination of your answers you like the most and see how that plays out as a story in your head.

Most of the examples we have used in this section have been from movies. But these goals are just as important in short form and episodic television. In the pilot episode of *Rick and Morty*, Rick wants to bring back Mega Tree Seeds from another dimension. SpongeBob might be delivering a pizza or passing his boating exam. In each case, it is the specific physical goal that is driving the story.

Chapter 3

OBSTACLES

Let's start with a bold statement.

If you don't have any obstacles you don't have a story.

All stories have obstacles for characters to overcome; whether we are talking about an epic saga or a short you are making for YouTube. If it's a story, you will need obstacles. While a goal drives your story, it's the obstacles that make it interesting.

Try to imagine a goal without an obstacle. Let's just say that we have a character, we'll call her Lou, and Lou's goal is to make a cup of coffee. Pretty straightforward, especially if she works in a coffee shop and she has all the necessary tools and ingredients in hand. If there's a coffee machine, she probably just needs to pour the coffee into a cup. So, we have a character and a goal. But we are left with a pretty uninteresting story—an animated short where someone pours coffee into a cup.

Now let's say that Lou goes to make the coffee and realizes that there is no coffee in the shop. We now have an obstacle to overcome and a bit more of a story, but still, it's not much of an obstacle and not much of a story. So, let's stack up the obstacles a bit more. What if there is an irate customer in the shop? He's fed up with Lou's bad service and won't leave till he gets his coffee—it's the only coffee shop for miles. She's also looking after the manager's children and Lou promised her that she wouldn't leave them unattended. Lou wants to run down the road to the shop, but the kids are refusing to come with her. She tries calling a friend and asking if they could bring her some coffee but she can't get a signal on her phone. Lou is still working out how to get some coffee when there is a power cut. She tries to explain this to the irate customer, but he is convinced she shut down the power herself to get him out of the shop. The irate customer, now suffering from caffeine withdrawal, turns apoplectic. He breaks a leg off one of the tables and threatens to smash the whole place up if he doesn't get his coffee.

That might be an extreme example, but you can see that we started off with a simple goal, but no obstacles. As we started to layer on the obstacles the story gained potential.

Let us tell you about one of Paul's first animations. This was intended to be a two-minute short that was going to be animated with clay on a friend's dining room table. The story was simple. There was a Buddhist monk trying to meditate. As he sat down, a chicken wandered past and started clucking. The monk's eyes open, and we can see that it's irritating him. He wants to meditate and the chicken is putting him off. We have an obstacle, the chicken. He needs to get rid of the chicken in order to meditate. What follows is a descent into violence as the monk tries to get rid of the chicken, eventually killing it with a huge hammer—such is his journey to inner peace.

This is a demonstration of one of the simplest stories you could ever tell. It would have been only two minutes long, but there was still a central character and an obstacle for him to overcome. Without the chicken, you would just be watching a monk meditate. That would be easy to animate, perhaps serene to watch, but wouldn't have been very entertaining.

Now that you are starting to understand the importance of obstacles in stories, it's worth spending some time and thinking about the different types of obstacles that can appear in your stories. These obstacles can range from a small obstacle within a scene to the huge obstacles that go across an entire movie, and they fall into two main categories. These are the obstacles that come from outside a character and obstacles that come from within.

External Obstacles

To emphasize the importance of external obstacles, it is worth thinking about the history of animated film. Television shows such as sitcoms have their roots in theater and radio; they rely very much on the spoken word, whereas animated movies started off in the era of silent film. If you look back at the early animations of Max and Dave Fleischer or *Newman Theater's Laugh-O-gram's* (some of Walt Disney's early animations), they had no dialogue. It was possible to put some speech bubbles or dialogue text on the screen in movies such as this, but the stories were visual and, as such, the obstacles that the characters faced had to be physical. With the advent of sound in movies, dialogue was now possible, but the physical aspects of the storytelling remained and animation is still dominated by stories with external obstacles for the characters to overcome. This goes back to our section on "why animation?" (see Chapter 1), characters talking would be easier and cheaper to film in live action than it would be to animate them.

There are a wide range of external obstacles that characters can face, and, like our previous coffee shop example, it is often worth layering on more than one type to keep the stakes high and your story interesting. But what are the different types of external conflict?

1. **The opponent.** As the name suggests, this is a character in direct opposition to the character you are following in your story. This can be an archvillain or just someone who is causing a small problem for your character. It is obvious that the Joker in *Batman: The Animated Series* is an opponent, but so is the slow-moving sloth in *Zootopia* when Judy Hopps is trying to get some information in a hurry.
2. **Natural.** Characters in animation will often face a natural obstacle. This can be anything from the desert in *Rango*, the stormy ocean in *Moana*, or even some rain if you're Barry in *Bee Movie*.
3. **Created.** Some of the obstacles that stand in our characters' way might not be natural. These obstacles can be created by the opponent, for example, the thorns that Maleficent magically produces to stop Prince Phillip in *Walt Disney's Sleeping Beauty* or they can be created by people or characters that we never see, like the road (or "river of death") in *Watership Down*. Other created obstacles can also come in the form of things like a magic spell or potion that somehow limits the character's abilities, like Tiana being turned into a frog (in *The Princess and the Frog*).

Internal Obstacles

Great animators have always had the ability to portray a wide range of emotions in their characters using both facial expressions and body language. These, however, were often simple or extreme emotions, making internal conflicts difficult to portray. We can see Wile E. Coyote's pain when he realizes he's about to plummet into the canyon, but it might be more difficult to portray an inner conflict, showing how he feels as a carnivore struggling to live on a bird-only diet when plant-based proteins are readily available.

In recent years, changes in technology have allowed modern animators to portray subtleties in emotion never imagined before. Just watch some of the facial expressions in *Missing Link*, these are getting close to the range and depth of emotion that live-action actors can portray. While most of the conflict in animation remains external, these advances in technology allow for more internal obstacles to play a part in storytelling.

There are two main types of internal obstacle.

1. **Fears.** Most of us have fears and ghosts from our past that haunt us and hold us back in some way, and the same can be true for animated characters. Whether it is Scooby Doo and his fear of ghosts (always a hindrance for a ghost hunter) or Shrek not being able to get over the fact that when all is said and done, he's an ugly ogre and he doesn't want to let people in emotionally.

    With this type of obstacle, it is important the fear be appropriate to the story. A fear is irrelevant if it doesn't challenge the character on his journey. If, for example, your character has a fear of public speaking, it is only relevant if they need to address an audience to achieve their goal.

2. **Promises.** This device is used to a much lesser extent, but can still be a useful way to make life difficult for your character. In our coffee shop example earlier, Lou's promise to look after the manager's children make it difficult for her to go out and get some more coffee. A promise that limits your character's ability can be useful, but it can also be frustrating for the audience if not used wisely. If breaking the promise is going to make a character's life a lot easier, there has to be a really strong reason for them to keep their promise. The last thing you want is the audience screaming "just break the promise!" at the screen.

Bonus Material

Some of you might have seen Chris Graves and Trey Parker's student film American History *(if you haven't, try and track it down—it's great!). If you have seen it, you might be saying that there aren't any obstacles in that film. And you'd be kind of right—although you might consider the characters who get killed to be obstacles to their killers. But while* American History *is a pseudo-story, it falls more under the category of art house documentary than a story in the truest sense of the word.*

While this might seem like an exception to the rule, we would argue that you can write a great animation without obstacles, but you can't tell a great story without them, and ultimately most animations are stories.

Thinky Time #5

Obstacles are so important to storytelling, that we ask ourselves on a nearly daily basis, "What obstacles can this goal throw up for our characters?" This exercise will help you to tune in to the obstacles that you see in animation.

1. Watch an episode from any animated TV series.
2. Identify the character that has the most significant goal in that episode.
3. List all the obstacles that the character needs to overcome in order to achieve that goal.
4. Once you have that list, look at the aforementioned categories and see which they fall under.

The more you do the aforementioned exercise, the more you should notice that animation tends to focus more on external obstacles than internal ones. As we said, it's a visual medium.

Chapter 4

CENTRAL CHARACTER

Most stories are primarily about one character. There can be lots of characters within a story, but there is usually just one primary (or central) character. What about movies like Disney's *Beauty and the Beast*? Surely that must have two central characters, the Beauty *and* the Beast? Both their characters are named in the title. Well yes, the story is about both Belle and the Beast. But Belle is the central character. Don't get us wrong; when you watch a movie or TV show, you will engage with and follow lots of characters over the course of the story, but usually there is still one main character.

Some of you, at this stage, may well be thinking of TV shows and movies with more than one central character. We ask you to put those thoughts on hold for a moment. We will come back to those exceptions in a little while. For the moment, we would like you to think about stories where there is only one central character. Some are easy to spot. There are no prizes for guessing who the central characters are in *The Bugs Bunny Show*, *Hong Kong Phooey*, *Shrek*, or *Kubo and the Two Strings* (note: it's not the two strings). If there is one character's name in the title, you can pretty much guess who the central character is.

Some titles are not so straightforward. What about *South Park*, *Flushed Away*, or *Hotel Transylvania*? These aren't obvious from the title, and sometimes, in movies like *Hotel Transylvania*, it's not obvious when you watch them either.

Identifying the Central Character

There are four basic questions you can ask that will help you identify the central character:

1. Who has the main goal that you follow through the story?
2. Who is the most proactive character in the story?

3. Which character spends the most time on screen?
4. Who changes or learns the most by the end of the story?

You might find that when you ask these questions, you get a few different answers as you go down the list. That's fine. But you will find that the same name will be the answer to the majority of those questions. Going back to *Beauty and the Beast*, Belle is the answer to the first three questions, but the Beast is the answer to the last. Conclusion, Belle is the central character in that story.

Who is the central character in *Hotel Transylvania*? Let's go through the four questions. Dracula has the act two goal of trying to get Jonathan out of the hotel and then has the act three goal of bringing him back again. His overarching goal is to protect his daughter. So, Dracula wins hands down on the goals. Dracula is proactive all the way through the movie in trying to achieve these goals, but he is also proactive in running the hotel. Another point to Dracula. Dracula spends the most time on screen (and is the first person we see) so again Dracula wins. Lastly, Dracula learns that humans aren't all bad, so Dracula changes the most in this movie as well. As you can see, *Hotel Transylvania* is one of the best examples of a movie with one central character as he is the answer to all four questions. The more you can achieve this in your own scripts, especially in the early days while you are learning the craft, the more successful your scripts will be.

You also might be thinking, what if the main characters in the story are allies? Surely then you're rooting for both characters. That's true, you are. But those characters will still be different in some way. If two characters think exactly the same thing about everything in the story, then one of them is redundant. Even in the closest alliance there will be conflict and differences of opinion. In these cases, one of the characters is still the central character while the other takes on a supporting role. In *Kung Fu Panda*, all of the warriors work together to defeat Tai Lung, but it is clearly Po's story—even if the title didn't give it away. For a further example of characters working together to achieve the same goal, look at the case studies on *Zootopia* and *Paw Patrol* in Chapter 9.

We hear lots of objections to the one central character principle when people pitch us ideas, enough for us to question ourselves about how important it is. Like we said, this is about tools not rules, so you don't have to stick to this principle, but what happens when you don't have a central character?

The Importance of One Central Character

When people watch an animated film or TV show, they are temporarily leaving the real world behind and going into another world. This happens in all fiction, but often more so in animation than live action. Even in a very realistic animation, you are still watching an artist's impression of the real world, not the world itself.

Let's look at *Family Guy*. On the surface, *Family Guy* is pretty much a standard family sitcom in the same vein as live-action sitcoms such as *Everybody Loves Raymond*, *The Middle*, or *Leave it to Beaver*. But *Family Guy* is animated, so it looks different. Most of the characters are human and they might look approximately like humans, but these are caricatures of real people, not actual people (see Figure 8). We also have a baby that is unlike any that you will see in the real world and a talking dog. As the viewer immerses themselves into this different world, they need something to latch onto, to be their guide in the world around them. It might seem like all of the characters are doing that job all at the same time, and they do all contribute, but it's easier to view this world through one person's eyes. We start to feel that character's emotions and we start to root for that character. If the viewpoint shifts back-and-forth from one character to another, that emotional engagement starts to get

Figure 8 *Family Guy*, "Blue Harvest", September 23, 2007.

watered down. The viewer is starting to think: Wait, do I think this? Or, do I think that? Live-action movies and television usually stick to one central character as well, but there are exceptions in movies such as *Magnolia*, *Pulp Fiction*, and *Love Actually*. These films shift viewpoints multiple times, but in the wacky world of animated stories this is much harder for an audience to follow and, therefore, it is much harder to find exceptions. It would seem that the more unusual the world of the story, the more important it is to stick to the fundamentals of storytelling—and having one central character is an important fundamental.

Now let's get back to *Family Guy*. Those of you who watch *Family Guy* might be thinking, "but wait a minute, I know for a fact that there is more than one central character in that show." You are right, and now that we have covered the basic principles of what makes a central character and why they are so important, we're going to examine one of the complexities of defining central characters.

A Plots and B Plots

An episode may have more than one plotline. These are called an A plot and a B plot if there are two of them. Two is the most common number, but it can be more (you could also have a C and a D plot). Each plotline is effectively its own story, and therefore will have its own central character and goal. Although you might be watching one episode of a show, you might be watching more than one story at the same time and each story will have its own goal.

Sometimes the two plots will overlap and interact with each other, but they can also be completely separate. It is important to remember that even when the two plots interact, they might be part of one bigger story, but they are still two different plotlines.

You will notice that one of the plots is called the A plot and the other is called the B plot. The A plot is the main drive of the episode and is the one that will take up the most screen time.

Central Character Case Study: Family Guy "Absolutely Babulous"

In the *Family Guy* episode *Absolutely Babulous*, we follow two plotlines. One in which we see Peter doing his best to fit into the world of Lois's parents and the other where we see Stewie trying to win a prize. In this case, Peter's storyline takes up the most screen time and is therefore the

A plot (this is common in *Family Guy* as Peter is the "family guy" in the title).

In this case, the A plot and the B plot are almost completely separate. Peter hardly interacts with Stewie in this episode, and they are rarely in the same scenes together so the two plotlines are easy to separate from one another.

The A plot is triggered when there is a fire at the family home and the Griffins are forced to go and live at the Pewterschmidt's house (Peter's father-in-law). Peter is forced to live in the world of his in-laws, a world of the rich and privileged. Peter does his best to fit in, but fails and ends up finding a place in the big Pewterschmidt house to drink alone. Then his mother-in-law (the Bab in the title) joins him. It turns out, she wasn't born into a rich family and misses being the girl she once was. Peter and Babs end up getting drunk together, and Babs rediscovers her old blue-collar self. But then, wanting to be true to her roots, Babs leaves Lois's father and goes back to the wild life she once lived. Lois blames Peter for her parents' separation and now Peter has to heal that rift. This gives Peter his goal.

So, Peter has the goal and is most proactive in this plotline; he is also in every A plot scene so has the most screen time too. In this case, nobody learns anything (except maybe that Peter will never get on with his father-in-law!) so Question 4 would be left blank. Peter is the answer to three out of the four questions and is clearly the central character in the A plot.

In the B plot, Stewie gets a medal for taking part in a preschool sports day. Then he discovers that all the trophies and medals he has ever received (including this one) have been for participation only; he didn't actually win them. Stewie is devastated; he only had to take part to get the medal and now feels that he has never accomplished anything.

Stewie resolves to achieve something for himself and sets out to win the Annual Quahog Pie Cook-Off. It's clear whose goal this is—Stewie wants to win the Cook-Off. But as we continue to try to identify who the central character in this plot is, it starts to get a little more tricky. Questions 2 and 3 ask, respectively, who is the most proactive in this story and who spends the most time on screen? Brian is helping Stewie throughout the story and is nearly as proactive as Stewie. He is also in all of the scenes, and the two characters share roughly the same amount of screen time. The answers to Questions 2 and 3 could be Stewie or Brian. If we were scoring it, we could give them half a point each. Then we get onto the last question. Who has changed or learnt the most? Stewie doesn't win, but he does come fifth. He wins a ribbon and learns what it feels like to achieve something and not just participate. It's Stewie again. Stewie is the answer to two of the questions and gets a half point in the other two. Stewie is clearly the central character in the B plot.

Thinky Time #6

Choose an episode from a long-running animated show that normally contains more than one plotline. If in doubt, we recommend *The Simpsons*, *Rick and Morty*, or *South Park* (if you accidentally pick a rare episode that has only one plotline, abandon it and try another one). Watch the episode and try to answer the following:

1. What are the various plotlines within that episode? Are there two or more than two? Which of these is the A plot?
2. What are the goals for each plotline?
3. Who are the central characters for each plotline?

By this stage, with your knowledge of goals, obstacles, and central characters, the answers to this should be relatively easy. This is still a worthwhile exercise to do. The more this thought process becomes part of your subconscious, the easier it is to write it yourself.

Chapter 5

THE THREE-ACT STRUCTURE

The three-act structure is something that writers love to talk about. We debate its value, when to use it and when it does not work. People will try to find movies that don't use it, to prove that it's not necessary while others will claim that it is a rule that must be adhered to. Some will argue the exact way in which to use the three acts, insisting on precise moments where the acts change. Every one of these stances is valid, but none should be stuck to with a sense of dogma.

The Importance of the Three-Act Structure

The three-act structure has been the main story structure in use since both TV and film began and animation is no exception. Since this one system of storytelling has been incredibly successful over the history of onscreen viewing, it is probably worth understanding it if you are going to be a writer of animation. Once you understand the three-act structure, it is so prevalent you will see it everywhere.

We were discussing the three-act structure with a musician/DJ once. He had been successful in the world of Dance Music and now wanted to spend his time writing. He considered himself an artist and believed in breaking down rules and doing things creatively that had never been done before. We had a conversation that went something like this.

```
                    DJ
        If the three-act structure is the
        way things are always written you
        should just tear up the rulebook.

The DJ mimes tearing up a piece of paper.
```

                          DJ (cont.)
Find a different way to do it! Every
time there's a rule in creativity,
smash it down, do something different.

                          US
Can we ask you a question? You're a
Pretty successful musician and DJ,
right?

                          DJ

Yup!

                          US

How many of your songs are in 4/4
time?

                          DJ

Huh?

                          US
How many of your songs use a rhythm
of four beats to the bar?

                          DJ
All of them . . .

                          US
Why did you stick to that rule? Why
didn't you just tear up the rulebook?

                          DJ
Cos that's what people dance to . . .

                          US
The case for the defence rests . . .

If you're a musician, you'll know that not every song composed has four beats to the bar. Classical music, rock, jazz and country, for example, all use unusual rhythms. There will even be experimental albums that use unique time signatures, or even ones that do not use rhythm at all. If you know nothing about music, talk to someone who does or do an internet search on 4/4 Time Signature (also called Common Time). The key piece of information you need is that most popular music is written in 4/4, or Common Time. If you want to be a successful writer of animation, you should probably avoid the three-act structure as often as Lennon and McCartney avoided 4/4 time. (If you want to examine this further, look at The Beatles songs that are not composed in 4/4 time and compare them to the success of the ones that are.)

Because the three-act structure is fundamentally important to storytelling, it holds a special place in this book. While most of the other "tools in the toolbox" will each have a chapter to itself, the three-act structure will go across four chapters. We will look at how the three acts work together to tell a story and then we will look at each act separately and show you how to use them in a story.

In this section, we will be using a lot of examples from well-known movies. That does not mean that the three-act structure is only used in feature length productions. It is just as common in a ten-minute animated series and sometimes even fits into animated shorts.

How Does the Three-Act Structure Work?

What we need to do now is break down how these three story "parts" work together to give us the most powerful stories. But what is the three-act structure?

The three-act structure gives us the changes in direction that a story takes, that work as a cohesive whole, in order for the characters to have completed a satisfying story journey.

Let's break that down and look at each part of that sentence separately.

The Changes in Direction That a Story Takes

You could think of these as the beginning, middle, and end of a story, but they are more than that. In act one, we see a character going in a particular direction in life and then something happens. This event changes the character's goals or intentions and the story changes direction. Act one ends and act two starts. The character pursues this new direction until another major event changes the direction of the story again. This signifies the end of act two and we go into the final act.

For example, in act one of a story, we might see a retired superhero enjoying the easy life; he no longer fights crime and is trying to get his golf handicap down to zero. Then, an archvillain escapes from prison and wants revenge. The direction of the hero's life has now changed. He has gone from pursuing a life of leisure to being a superhero again as he tries to protect himself from the machinations of the archvillain. When that change in direction happens, we move from act one to act two. After the hero battles the villain for a while, it turns out that the villain has a huge bomb that will destroy the city. Now we move from act two to act three as the hero's goal changes from trying to save himself, to trying to save the city. These changes in direction are how the story takes us through the three acts.

That Work as a Cohesive Whole

All three acts in a three-act structure work together. In *How to Train Your Dragon*, Hiccup's overarching desire is to be a valued member of the tribe, despite being smaller and weaker than the other Vikings. In the first act, Hiccup wants to kill a Night Fury because no other Viking has ever killed one. In act two, Hiccup is starting to befriend a Night Fury dragon that he calls Toothless. Now that he has made friends with a dragon, his goal changes. His act two goal is to complete "dragon training" by taming the dragons instead of killing them. In act three, Hiccup's goal is to save the dragons and the Vikings by uniting them and defeating Red Death, the Queen of the dragons. Each of these acts has a distinct goal, but they are made a cohesive whole by the theme of Hiccup wanting to be a valued member of the tribe. A goal he only attains at the end.

Sometimes movies and TV shows work as a series of different short stories, but that is not the three-act structure. *The Simpson's Treehouse of Horror* episodes are a perfect example of three separate short stories linked together but they are *not* the three-act structure.

In Order for the Characters to Have Completed
a Satisfying Story Journey

Over the course of the story, we will see the central character's life change as they go through a series of challenges that relate to a specific theme or event in that character's life. These challenges are not always played out in three acts. You can find stories that have two acts or four acts, but a two-act story will often feel like "something" is missing and a four-act story is often a step too far and can seem confusing. There is just a kind of magic that works when we tell stories over three acts. The changes in direction at the end of act one and act two seem to create a synergy that lifts the story to a higher level.

For clarity, we should state that these acts do not necessarily equate to the placement of ad breaks in broadcasting. Production executives, particularly when referring to one-hour TV shows, will often say that the story is four acts. This refers to the four parts of story when broadcast with three advert breaks in the body of the episode. In storytelling terms, this is usually still a three-act story structure with a break at the end of act one, in the middle of act two, and then at the end of act two.

When to Break the Rule

At the beginning of the book, we told you this was about "tools not rules." Then we told you all about how important the three-act structure was, so by now you might be thinking this one is a rule. No, it's just a very useful tool and one that you will probably use a lot. So much so, that we would say that it is worth mastering before you start writing stories that are not in the three-act structure.

Shows as popular as *The Simpsons*, *Family Guy*, and *SpongeBob SquarePants* often steer away from the three-act structure. Even a movie as successful as *Toy Story 3* (see Chapter 24) tells its story in four acts—hardly a subversive art house movie—but there are two things to remember about these exceptions. First, they are written by very accomplished writers, who have written a lot and have an incredible story instinct. Second, whether they are aware of it or not, these shows still use an act structure, it's just not always three acts. Remember the concept of the story changing direction? These are still act changes, whether there are five, six, or two of them. Often, the more "wacky" shows have more act changes; this is one of the reasons they seem bizarre! (If you want to check this out yourself, choose a couple of episodes of *Rick & Morty* at random and see how many direction changes are in the episode. You might hit on one with three acts, but chances are there will be more.)

The Three-Act Structure in Animation

Now one thing you may have noticed is that most on-screen stories use the three-act structure, so you might be wondering if it works differently when applied to animation. Well it does and it doesn't. There is no set rule that the three-act structure should be used in a different way when applied to an animated story, but when you dig a bit deeper, you find that animation tends to use act structure in a distinct way. As we go through each act in turn, you will find more of an emphasis on the "physical, tickable goals" for each act. By keeping these the focus of your story, you are more likely to maintain the fast-paced, visual style associated with animation and keep the drive of your story going. It is this form of act structure we will focus on as we proceed.

Now we have looked at how the three-act structure works as a whole, we are going to move on to look at each act separately. To understand the next chapters, and to use them as effective tools, especially in animation, you need to have a solid grasp of how goals in storytelling work. If you skipped the chapter on goals, we recommend you read it again now (it is a short chapter!).

Chapter 6

ACT TWO

This might seem like the wrong order, but we're going to examine the second act before we get to the first one. Act two is the central drive of your story and can often make up as much as half of the total screen time. It is the backbone of your story, and you need to get this act to work or the rest of the story will fall flat.

Act two obviously follows act one, and we know from the previous chapter that means that there has been a change in direction for our lead character. But what does that change in direction mean? It normally means that our central character is now pursuing a specific, physical, and tickable goal. The start of that pursuit signifies the end of act one and the beginning of act two.

Just to clarify, a character might have a goal or an emotional need from the beginning of the story. They might have several goals in life, but

A strong act two follows a central character pursuing a specific, physical and tickable goal.

In *Moana*, this is when Moana sets off to get Maui to return the heart to Te Fiti. This is physical as it requires an arduous journey. It is also specific as she has been asked to take a particular item to a specific person. And it is definitely tickable; she can't tick that box until the heart has been returned.

In *Kung Fu Panda*, act two begins when Po starts his training to become the Dragon Warrior. Kung Fu training is definitely physical. It's specific; he hasn't set a goal to be "really good at Kung Fu," he is to become the Dragon Warrior. And we know it's tickable as the moment is symbolized by the presentation of the Dragon Scroll. No Dragon Scroll, no Dragon Warrior.

The Functions of Act Two

Now that our central character is working toward a specific goal, let's look at the three main functions of this act:

1. To show our central character actively pursuing their goal
2. To raise the stakes for our central character in the story
3. To increase the pace of the story by showing our central character facing increasingly difficult situations and overcoming them

Let's look at each of the above points separately.

To Show Our Central Character Actively Pursuing Their Goal

This one sounds simple, but there is an art to getting this right. The key word here is "actively." It's very easy to have other characters present information or opportunities to your central character, but the more they need to do things for themselves, the more the audience will be invested in the story.

When *Moana* sets off to complete her goal, she only has one companion with her. A stupid chicken. An animal that is great comedy relief in the story, but, at least for act two, is more of a burden than a blessing. Then, when she finally meets Maui, he doesn't want to help her pursue her goal. He gives her more obstacles, not assistance.

A powerful thing happens when we see a character overcome obstacles for themselves. As an audience, we bond with them. We start to see things from their point of view. This in turn gets us to engage with the story. We start to root for the character, which makes us share both their triumphs and defeats. Much of this is lost if we make their journey too easy.

Raise the Stakes for Our Central Character

As we move into act two, something must be at stake for our character. If there are no consequences to not achieving the goal, then there is nothing to engage the audience. Moana must return the heart or the darkness will continue to poison the island. If Po doesn't become the Dragon Warrior, then Tai Lung will exact his revenge. If Woody doesn't get Buzz back to Andy's before he moves house, they will never see him again.

Once the character crosses into act two, their life can never be the same. They will either achieve their goal and their life will be better or they will fail and their life will be worse. It cannot be that they could just abandon their goal and everything will go back to how it was before.

It is important to note here that sometimes this can be a simple emotional stake. Animation is often targeted at children or family audiences so we might not always want to use life or death as a threat to our character. In *101 Dalmatians*, Cruella De Vil wants to make a fur coat out of Pongo and Perdita's puppies—a seriously high stake! But in *Rugrats* we see the characters experiencing the everyday life of small children. In this show, we see characters dealing with stakes such as getting the cereal you want for breakfast or worrying about your booster shot. While they might seem like great adventures in the babies' minds, they are usually safe from physical harm.

To Increase the Pace of the Story by Showing Our Central Character Facing Increasingly Difficult Situations and Overcoming Them

We have a clearly defined goal and the stakes are set. As act two progresses, the character will face a series of obstacles to achieving that goal. These obstacles should increase in difficulty as the story moves forward. This increase can come from the obstacles becoming more problematic, more hazardous, or through the introduction of a deadline. Sometimes all three.

In the second act of *Coco*, Miguel's goal is to get the blessing of a family member so that he can return to the land of the living before sunrise—if he fails, Miguel will become one of the dead. We have our first deadline—Miguel must attain his goal before sunrise. Then, as we move through the act, the physical obstacles to the goal increase. Believing his great-great-grandfather, Ernesto, is his best chance to receive the blessing, he sets off to find him. But Ernesto is very famous in the Land of the Dead, and getting to him is tricky. Then, when Ernesto turns against him, things get harder. Next, Miguel discovers that Héctor is his real great-great-grandfather, who was murdered by Ernesto. This is a complication for Miguel, and the stakes in the story have just gone up. Now, if he returns to the land of the living without a photo of Héctor, then Héctor will be forgotten and cease to exist. Unfortunately, the evil Ernesto now has the photo. As Héctor starts to weaken, nearly forgotten in the land of the living, Miguel's final challenge is to retrieve the photo and get the blessing before Héctor disappears. The obstacles get bigger, but the tension is also increased by the weakening of Héctor (see Figure 9), which gives us a very visual ticking clock that runs alongside the act two obstacles.

Figure 9 *Coco*, October 20, 2017.

It's important to place these challenges in the right order. If the difficulties the character is facing get smaller as they progress, the story will slow down and the audience will lose interest. The number of challenges that the character faces will dictate the length of the story. In a very short story, you may only need a couple of simple challenges; if you are writing a feature film, you will need several, and each one could be quite complex.

The best way to see how this works is through an exercise.

Thinky Time #7

We know what it's like when you read a book like this. You don't really want to do the exercises and you might read them but not really engage with them. We encourage you to do all of the Thinky Times to get as much as you can from this book. But if you were to do just one, we implore you to do this one. Poor act two plotting is probably the biggest weakness in animation writers today.

If you have your own idea for a story that you want to plot out here, then use that idea. If not, we have provided a story idea in the following text.

Let's just say that you've started working on a show that's a medical drama with robots. It's just like ER but all the patients and doctors are robots. The producers have asked you to write an episode centered around a robot that needs some kind of a transplant. After some brainstorming, you decide that in your story there is a robot that needs a new processor. The team has located a donor robot, but it's in a different robot hospital on the other side of Robot City. Let's say our main character is a new junior robot doctor called B73. Your act two goal is to retrieve the processor and bring it back to the hospital before the damaged robot shuts down completely. We will imagine that this is for a ten-minute episode and you will need the plot to escalate three times. Now, plot out act two using the following four steps.

1. Come up with five potential challenges that B73 might need to overcome as he tries to bring the processor back. If nothing happens on his journey, you haven't got much of a story. These challenges can be things that go wrong, people that create problems for him, or even opponents trying to stop him for some reason.
2. Choose the three challenges that you like the best or excite you the most.
3. Put the three challenges into order from the easiest for B73 to overcome to the most difficult. If they all seem roughly equal and you're not sure which order to put them in, try building some of them up. If you thought that B73 might take a rocket bike to the hospital and it broke down, what happens if you evolve it a little? What if the rocket bike got stolen? What if it got stolen with the needed processor on board?
4. Once you have three story "beats" (these are the incidents that will make up the rhythm of your story) and they're in an order you're happy with, play the story out in your mind. How does it feel? It might need some tweaks, but it should feel like a pretty good story.

Look back at this last four-step process. You started with the bare bones of an idea, you did a short exercise, and suddenly you have the backbone of a solid story. This may seem simple, but it is powerful. We use this process on nearly every story we write.

The End of Act Two

Act two ends when the story turns in a new direction. Often, this can be in the form of a new goal, but just as often it can involve the central character facing disaster and giving up on their act two goal altogether. It can also be both of those things at the same time.

In the previous chapter, we saw that in *How to Train Your Dragon* Hiccup's goal for act two was to tame the dragons. When his father chains up Toothless, the dragon Hiccup has befriended, and plans to use him to find the dragons' nest, Hiccup has to do more than just tame the dragons if he is going to save his friend, so his goal changes. His new goal is to unite the dragons and the Vikings and defeat the biggest dragon of all, Red Death.

In contrast to this, in *Sing* we see that Buster Moon's goal in act three is the same as it is in act two—to put on a great show. These two acts are separated by the moment when Buster gives up on his dream entirely. At the end of act two, not only do the contestants think he's a fraud when they discover that he hasn't got the promised prize money, his whole theater is destroyed by a flood. While his goal doesn't change, at the end of act two, he is as far away from achieving his goal as possible.

Challenges of Act Two

Act two is usually the longest of the three acts and is often difficult to sustain. The constant need to increase the stakes and make the problems more challenging make it hard to plot, especially in a feature film. The way to tackle this challenge is to make sure that you get the specific, physical, and tickable goal right. Ask yourself the question, "Does this goal create enough for the characters to do?" Be brutally honest with yourself; if the answer is "no," keep thinking until you are sure your act two goal will provide you with enough story material.

A Word of Warning

It's easy to fall in love with a great opening you have in mind, or a brilliant finale. Don't be tempted to try to engineer an act two that accommodates that show stopping scene you've got planned. Get act two right first! Chances are that great scene will still work by the time you get to the final draft, it might need to change slightly, but in our experience that change will make the whole thing better.

Chapter 7

ACT ONE

Act one is the story's setup. It gives us all the information we need to make sense of everything else that's going to happen. In a feature, it usually takes up about a quarter of the total screen time, so for a two-hour movie the first act will usually last about a half hour. In a ten-minute TV show, ideally act one will end at around two-and-a-half minutes into the episode, although it often ends up being a little longer as it's hard to establish the whole setup in less than three minutes.

The Functions of Act One

1. It introduces your central character and most of the other main characters that will recur throughout the story.
2. It sets up the world of your story.
3. It reveals the main problems that exist in the character's life and creates sympathy for him or her.
4. It states the main goal of our character and the specific goal of act two. As soon as our character embarks on the act two goal, act one is finished and we're into the central core of our story.

Let's look at each of these points in a little more detail.

It Introduces Your Central Character and Most of the Other Main Characters That Will Recur throughout the Story

The audience need to know who the central character is as soon as possible. In Chapters 4 and 10, we will look at some devices that will help you to create an audience connection with your central character, but you can often tell who it is just by the way they are introduced. When you watch animated movies, make a mental note of how they introduce the main character. Watch the camera angles and the shots they use. Do they start with the feet? Or maybe a close-up of the eyes? If it's on the screen, it's on the page; so use this cinematic language as much as you can.

Most stories have more than one character. Some of these characters will recur throughout the story and some will appear in only certain scenes. Ideally, in act one a story should introduce as many of the recurring characters as possible before the act two goal starts. In the first act of *Toy Story*, we meet all of Andy's toys, we meet Andy and his family, and we're introduced to the sinister kid next door, if only from a distance (but we could probably guess that he would come back later).

It Sets up the World of Your Story

In animation, your world can be anything. It can be under the sea or in outer space. The characters can be humans, talking vegetables, or literally anything you can think of. These worlds can be complex, but they also need to be consistent and, most importantly of all, they need to be understood by your audience.

There are three key elements to consider about the world of your story:

1. The community
2. The environment
3. The genre

The community we have touched on in the previous point. These are the characters that inhabit your central character's world at the start of the story. In *Toy Story*, it is all the toys in Andy's toy box. In *Beauty and the Beast*, it's all the people in the village, but it's also all the characters that live in the castle as the castle will become the community for much of the story.

The environment of the story refers to the place all the characters live. Is this a world of Superheroes or Pirates? Do they live under the sea? Are they toys? Is it medieval times? Maybe medieval times with a few modern accessories? Are the subtleties of the world more complicated than that? It could be that the story is set in prehistoric times and the characters are cave people, but the worlds of *The Croods* and *The Flintstones* are significantly different. The audience needs to understand the rules and intricacies of the story world by the time act one has finished. To go back to our caveman example, *The Croods* inhabit a relatively realistic stone-age world when compared to the world of the *The Flintstones*. See Figures 10 and 11 for a comparison. Once that world has been established, the writers need to stick to the rules that they have created for that world. If the sitcom-like scene that we see in Figure 11 turned up in act two of *The Croods*, the audience wouldn't buy it; it just isn't part of the world established in act one.

Figure 10 *The Croods*, March 22, 2013.

Figure 11 *The Flintstones*, "Hot Lips Hannigan", October 7, 1960.

Genre is a big subject. There are plenty of books just about this one subject. There are great advantages to mastering genre, but you don't need to understand it all to use genre well. The audience understands genre, even if they don't realize that they do. We are exposed to genre as soon as we start watching TV and film. Imagine the opening of a movie. We see a desert landscape, dotted with cacti. The camera moves in on a dusty wooden shack with a horse tied outside. Tumbleweed blows across the screen and vultures circle overhead. Just a few images and a few seconds of screen time and we can work out that we're probably in a Western. Just by watching TV shows and movies in the genre you are writing for, you will start to absorb the language of these films.

This might seem like a lot of information that needs to be conveyed to establish the world of your story, but this is animation and animation is a visual medium. It is amazing how fast the audience will pick up on information that they see. If we go back to *The Flintstones* and look at the original series, first broadcast in 1960, we can see how quickly we understand quite a complicated premise. In the first episode, they didn't have lyrics in the theme song yet, so we have no words to tell us what the story is. Remember, this is the first ever episode, so audiences don't know what to expect. The opening image is of a man who seems to be driving home from work, but he's dressed like a caveman and all the cars are made from rocks and logs. He drives through the city and we see an environment that seems a little bit like a modern world, but it has a stone-age twist—we see a dinosaur being used as a fire engine and a tailor shop with another dinosaur acting as the stairs to the entrance way. Less than thirty seconds in and the audience will already understand that this is a modern story set in a mock prehistoric world. If they haven't worked out that it's a comedy yet, they are about to find out the exact type of comedy it is. At the end of the credits, we see the caveman's wife waiting for him with the dinner she has made. He kisses her on the cheek and then sits down with his food to watch some TV. Not that acceptable in the twenty-first century, but in the 1960s this was a standard setup for a sitcom. In less than a minute with no dialogue, we know the world, we know the genre, and we can guess that the caveman and his wife will be the main characters.

*It Reveals the Main Problems That Exist in the Character's
Life and Creates Sympathy for Him or Her*

Most stories start with a problem. It doesn't have to be a big problem yet, but things aren't usually perfect for our central character. If they are, they don't stay perfect for long. Watching a group of people being happy and just getting along is great in real life, but most people won't pay to watch it. Whatever the difficulty or challenge, it gives our character some conflict to work against—and conflict drives story. It also creates sympathy for the character, especially if it's a situation we recognize. We wouldn't like to be in that predicament ourselves so we start to bond emotionally with the person who is in it.

In the opening of *Toy Story 3*, Andy is going off to college and the toys are all facing the prospect that he doesn't want to play with them anymore, but also that they are about to be split up. Some will be put in the attic and some will be sent to daycare. In *Beauty and the Beast*, we learn that Belle is not supposed to read or have an imagination. The local villagers think she is odd and the local muscular—but vacuous—hunk wants to marry her. It's clear that she wants adventure but her destiny is to settle down and have children, probably with a guy that doesn't understand her. By the end of her first song, we understand a lot of Belle's problems and this creates sympathy for her.

These difficulties are set up very quickly and help us to relate to the characters. You may also notice that the problem at this stage of the story relates thematically to the main issue that they will face later. Belle gets her adventure and discovers a magical castle. Woody sets off to bring his friends back together again—with someone who will play with them. This is kind of a chicken-and-egg situation; which has the writer planned first? Was it the predicament at the beginning of the story or the main drive of act two? Whenever you watch a movie or an episode of an animated TV series, observe how these things are connected. Think about the main issue in the central character's life at the beginning and see how it relates thematically, to the main drive of the story.

It States the Main Goal of Our Character
and the Specific Goal of Act Two

We have already seen the importance of the act two goal. It is also important to be aware that our central character may also have an overarching goal that spans the length of the story. This is often less specific (and 'tickable') and can be more of an emotional need for our character. You might also notice that it will relate to the problem that exists for the character at the beginning of the story (referred to in the previous segment). We're getting into a complex theoretical area here, so let's look at an example to clarify.

At the beginning of *Kung Fu Panda*, Po works in his adoptive father's noodle restaurant. This might not seem like a problem, but Po really wants to learn Kung Fu; he wants to learn it so much that he literally dreams about it. His father however, is expecting him to learn the secret family recipe and take over the noodle bar. His father even tells him that he will be fulfilling his destiny by taking over the restaurant. To drive the point home, the writers create an image of how Po sees his future (see Figure 12). Po's father tells him that "we all have our place in this world" and Po's is waiting on tables. This is a problem people can relate to. Most people watching will be thinking, "yeah, I'd rather do Kung Fu than work in the noodle place." The writers have established a problem and an overarching goal. The problem is that his father expects him to pursue a career that he doesn't want, and his overarching goal is to learn Kung Fu. Later, when Po is selected to train to be the Dragon Warrior, we have a new specific goal that launches us in to act two.

Notice how the problem, the overarching goal and the act two goal work together. At the beginning, Po dreams of learning Kung Fu. This is fairly vague as a goal; he doesn't say what level he wants to be or where he wants to learn it, but it doesn't matter at this stage. This is Po's emotional need, not the physical, tickable goal required for act two (there will be more about emotional need in Chapter 11). The big problem for Po is that he must work at the noodle bar so he can't learn Kung Fu. It might also be worth adding that being a panda might be

Figure 12 *Kung Fu Panda*, June 6, 2008.

another problem for Po; pandas do not seem to possess the qualities you would expect in a great martial artist.

Challenges of Act One

There is a lot of information to set up. This means that it's easy to fill up with content, but can be difficult to make entertaining. And, if you don't make it entertaining, no one will still be reading (or watching) when you get to act two.

This is where goals can help. Try setting a mini physical, tickable goal that drives your central character until they reach the act two turning point. This can keep the visual elements of act one moving, without getting completely weighed down by the setup of your story. (Note: this tool is not unique to animation, but it is employed in animation a lot more than in live-action film and television.)

Chapter 8

ACT THREE

The final act. Like act one, this act makes up roughly a quarter of the total screen time in a feature film. This may vary in shorter forms, but as this is the most exciting part of your story, you don't want it to be too short or too easy for the lead character. In this act, you will see them face their final conflict or the biggest obstacle so far.

The Functions of Act Three

1. To be the most exciting or dramatic part of your story.
2. Provide a satisfying ending that makes everyone glad they watched your movie or show.

Now, let's look at those two points in a bit more detail.

To Be the Most Exciting or Dramatic Part of Your Story

If you have created a great act two, it can be hard to make this even more exciting or dramatic. The key thing to remember is that act three starts with a change in direction to the story. When you plot out your three acts, the change in direction for your story should automatically do at least one of the following three—maybe even all three:

1. Make your character face the biggest challenge or obstacle of the story so far.
2. Increase the consequences of failure.
3. Tighten the deadline.

As your character moves into the final act, the drama will increase if the obstacle your character faces is bigger. In *Hotel Transylvania 2*, this is where Dracula's father, the icy-cold and intimidating Vlad, turns up. In *Kung Fu Panda*, Po must face the fearsome Tai Lung on his own. In the *Triplets of Belleville* (*Belleville Rendez-vous* in some territories), this is the big escape sequence at the end. In each of these cases, we see the central character facing the biggest obstacle so far, they will sometimes be facing it alone and will usually appear outgunned.

This act change should also increase the consequences of failure. In *Hotel Transylvania 2*, when Vlad arrives, we move from Dracula desperately wanting his grandson to be a vampire to lives being at stake. In the *Triplets of Belleville*, Madame Souza goes from wanting to find her son to breaking him out of a Mob establishment and having to escape their henchmen.

The tension can also be increased if the time that our hero has left to achieve their goal decreases. This can be a literal ticking clock, like a time bomb counting down or a metaphorical version of it. We see this in movies such as *Shrek* or *Beauty and the Beast*, whether it's Shrek needing to get to Fiona before she marries Lord Farquaad or the Beast earning the love of another before the last petal falls. The deadline can also be something less tangible. In *The Curse of the Were-Rabbit*, we see Victor Quartermaine hunting down Wallace, and in the *Triplets of Belleville* we see the Mob henchmen closing in on Madame Souza. In both cases, although there is no definite deadline, the villains are getting progressively closer to permanently foiling our hero, and, therefore, the tension is increased. Anything that makes the success of our character more urgent will increase the drama of the final act.

Provide a Satisfying Ending That Makes Everyone
Glad They Watched Your Movie or Show

We're at the end of the movie. The central character has achieved their goal, or maybe failed if it has a downbeat ending, and we're about to see a new beginning. In the final scenes, we normally get a glimpse of what life in the future is going to be like for the main characters. We see all the plotlines and issues resolved. But these don't necessarily give us a satisfying ending. How does your hero defeat the villain or overcome their biggest obstacle? If your character just has the ability or strength to do it, the act three challenge probably isn't big enough and the ending might just seem convenient.

If the ending to your story isn't having the big impact you would like, you can often make it stronger by using the tool we call "callback and payoff."

Callback and payoff is a storytelling device that refers to using something that has happened earlier in the story that pays off in the final scenes. This can work in a number of different ways. It can be an item that we see, or a piece of information that the audience is given; it can even be something that the character is trying to learn how to do, but hasn't yet succeeded at. The important thing is that when it first appears, the callback device shouldn't seem overly relevant to the story; then, when this "pays off" later, it should take the audience by surprise—ideally followed by them all thinking, "Of course! I should have seen that coming!"

In *The Incredibles*, we hear early on in the movie of the dangers of wearing a cape. Mr. Incredible wants a cape on his new suit but Edna, the suit designer, tells him that he can't have one. She regales him with the stories of heroes who have come to a sticky end when their capes snagged on something. It's a funny scene, and, to the untrained eye, it just seems like the comedy is the reason that the scene is there. But then, near the end of the movie, Syndrome's cape gets sucked into a jet engine bringing about his demise. As a member of the audience, we mentally callback to the information that we had from Edna when the cape/jet engine scenario pays off.

Using the callback is often as simple as going back through your story to see what has happened so far. Is there anything that has appeared that will be useful in the end? It is amazing how many times that the required "thing" is already there, nestled in the story ready to be called-back to.

Bonus Material: A Cure for Coincidence

Coincidences happen in real life all the time. We might run into a next-door neighbor while on vacation or see an old school friend that you were just talking about but hadn't seen for years. These things happen. The problem is, they can't happen so much in stories; audiences don't tend to believe them. Just the right person turning up at just the right time might happen in the real world, but an audience watching this in an animated story can feel cheated. Callback and payoff is a cure for that. If you need that coincidental event at the end of your movie or episode, go back and set it up early on in your story. If done well, your "coincidence" evolves from being a bit too convenient to a clever and satisfying plot turn.

Challenges of Act Three

In act three, the writer is walking a tightrope, trying to keep the challenges big enough to keep the audience on the edge of their seat while at the same time keeping it believable that the hero succeeds.

While we recommend plotting act two first, remember that whatever you plotted is not written in stone; you will find yourself going back-and-forth between the acts trying to make the script work as a cohesive whole. Plotting a good story is like trying to make a sculpture out of jelly, it doesn't quite behave. Chances are, your script will need constant molding and remolding as things change. Just say, you've decided that the best way for your villainous pirate captain to be defeated is to have him eaten by a crocodile; if there haven't been any crocodiles in the story so far, then that would come too much out of the blue. You would need to thread in a crocodile plot to make it truly satisfying. Watch *Peter Pan* and imagine how unsatisfying the ending would be if that was the first time the crocodile appeared. You can see a similar thing, again with a crocodile, in the Aardman animation *A Matter of Loaf and Death*. Once you know the ending you want, go back through the script and plot the necessary changes to make it work.

Chapter 9

THREE-ACT STRUCTURE CASE STUDIES

To see how the three-act structure works in different forms, we are going to work through an in-depth study of both Disney's *Zootopia* (known as *Zootropolis* in some territories) and an episode of *Paw Patrol*. *Zootopia* is one of the more complex stories you'll find in animation; it takes place in a fantasy world with a highly original and intricate social structure. It is also a densely plotted conspiracy thriller and contains deep themes about prejudice and the damage it does to society. *Paw Patrol* on the other hand uses short and simple stories for a young audience but is hugely successful.

Three-Act Structure Case Study 1: Zootopia

Act One

Let's look at the four functions of the first act as they work in *Zootopia*.

First, the characters. In the opening scene, we meet Judy Hopps, a rabbit, and it's clear from the beginning that she is going to be our central character. We learn very quickly that she wants to be a cop in Zootropolis, but we also learn that her parents don't want her to be a cop and encourage her to not have any goals. Here we see Judy's problem and her overarching goal working together to set up the direction of the story. Later, when we get to act two, we will see how achieving the act two goal links in with these plot points.

Next, we learn that one of Judy's character traits is that she doesn't know when to quit. This is something that, later in the story, will drive her on against impossible odds.

As act one progresses, we also meet the police chief, the mayor, and the assistant mayor, all of whom are key characters. More importantly, we meet Nick Wilde, the con artist fox who will start off as Judy's opponent but will become her ally.

Next, the movie sets up the world in which the story is set, and this script does it with brilliant efficiency. Zootopia and, more specifically, the city of Zootropolis are perhaps the most complicated worlds you will see in any movie —not just an animated one. But we learn about the history of predators and prey, and we learn about the different districts of the city and how the creatures manage to coexist, from Sahara Square to Tundra Town. More importantly, we see it all visually. If you watch the scene when Judy arrives in Zootopia Central Station, you see everything you need to know about how this world works (see Figures 13 and 14).

We also learn about genre in the opening as well. In the opening scene with the school play, we see Judy's blood-soaked portrayal of the history of Zootopia and it's funny. This is a comedy. We also see the dramatic scene where she tries to stand up to the local bully, Gideon Grey, so this is going to have some drama. A little later, but still in act one, we see her doing some detective work when she spots Nick Wilde's pawsicle hustle—so it's a detective movie too.

Third, we can see the problems that Judy Hopps is going to have to overcome in her quest to be a Zootopia cop. There is a prejudice against her being a rabbit—a rabbit has never made it as a cop. Her parents don't want her to be a cop. She seems to be the smallest and weakest cadet at the police academy. When she becomes a cop, the chief doesn't want her there and he makes her work as a meter maid. None of this is an easy journey—fortunately, Judy doesn't know when to quit!

Figure 13 *Zootopia*, March 4, 2016.

Figure 14 *Zootopia*, March 4, 2016.

Lastly, the act two goal. We know from quite early on that Judy Hopps wants to be a cop. That is her overarching goal within the story, but this goal leads us to a more specific goal. The goal that will provide the real action. This is going to be a missing person mystery. Let's look at how act one ends:

```
                    CHIEF BOGO
        I will give you forty-eight hours . . .


                    JUDY HOPPS
                   (triumphantly)
        YES!!


                    CHIEF BOGO
        That's two days to find Emmitt Otterton . . .


                    JUDY HOPPS
        Okay . . .
```

And that's it! Judy Hopps must find Emmitt Otterton in forty-eight hours. As soon as we know the specific goal for act two, act one ends and act two begins. But think of how specific this goal is. We learn early on that there are a lot of missing animals in Zootopia; the goal could be to crack the case of the missing animals. That would seem like a perfectly valid goal, but, normally, in storytelling, the more specific the goal, the better it is. What's more specific than crack the case of the missing animals? Find one particular animal in a set time frame. Remember the tip about the "tickable" physical goal? This goal is really easy to tick off. At the end of forty-eight hours, either Emmitt Otterton is found or he isn't, and Judy will either be able to tick that goal or not. That's what makes this a great goal for this story.

Before we go onto act two, we want you to think about how the writers of Zootopia achieved all these things so quickly and in an entertaining way. Earlier we said that you had to understand goals to grasp the three-act structure. This is why. During act one, we were watching Judy trying to achieve her goal of becoming a cop, we were engaged in the story, and we weren't just watching information being presented to us. Judy Hopps is overcoming a series of smaller goals on her journey to becoming the first bunny cop. Whether she is dealing with the local bully's prejudice, fighting a rhino in the academy boxing ring, or trying to give out 200 parking tickets before lunch, we were watching Judy achieving mini-goals and overcoming difficulties in order to achieve her main overarching goal. The problem is, she never quite achieves it—not till much later-on anyway. As we hear from her parents when they see she is on meter maid duty: She's not a real cop! Despite everything she's been through.

Act Two

Act one ends when we know the physical goal for act two. But act two also starts with something at stake. Not only must she find Emmett Otterton, she is told she must do it in forty-eight hours or resign. Remember, one of the functions of act two is to raise the stakes. Zootopia does that straight away. Judy's lifelong ambition is to be a cop, she's finally got her chance, but if she doesn't find Emmett in two days, she must resign and she will never achieve her dream. The stakes are high.

This increase in stake is important. A story is always stronger if your character can't turn back from the goal. The moment your central character crosses over into act two, it should be difficult or, better yet, impossible for them to go back to life the way it was before.

Let's focus on this for a moment. What if Judy doesn't achieve her goal? Forty-eight hours are up and she hasn't found the missing otter? Judy could resign, then presumably she would go back to work on her parents' farm and live a simple life free from crime and excitement. Maybe she could plead with Chief Bogo to keep her job, and she would have to agree to be a meter maid for the rest of her life. As a viewer, neither of these outcomes are satisfying, and you just don't want them to happen, which makes you invested in Judy's act two goal.

Now often, especially in longer forms, the stakes are raised more than once. As Judy's investigation continues, her life is in danger several times; from Mr. Big's polar bear henchmen, who are going to "ice" her, to the jaguar, who goes "savage," and not forgetting the timber wolves on security when she sneaks into the mysterious compound. Losing her job is a high stake, losing her life is even higher.

It is worth noting here that while the threat to life is a common stake raiser, it is not the only way to raise the stakes. In *Toy Story*, for example, the biggest stake perhaps is that Woody will never see Andy again. A stake that goes up when the family is about to move home. Another important factor when raising the stakes for a character is that a lot of animation is written for a very young audience and the possibility of a character dying isn't always appropriate.

The other main function of act two is to show our protagonist facing increasingly difficult challenges and overcoming them. If our goal for act two is easy to attain, then the story won't be engaging. In *Zootopia*, we know that finding Emmett is going to be difficult; there are fourteen missing predators and the police so far have drawn a blank on all of them—this mystery has so far defeated the entire police department. But then, Clawhauser gives Judy the case file and points out that there are no leads and no witnesses, and she doesn't have access to the computer system yet, so she has no resources.

Judy's first challenge is where to start. She has one photo of the missing Emmett so she scrutinizes that, which gives her the first lead— she has discovered the identity of the last person to have seen Emmett. Unfortunately, it's Nick Wilde, her opponent in act one. Judy's next obstacle is coercing Nick to help her. Once she has Nick on her side, the obstacles keep coming. They find out the license plate number of the car, they trace the car, they break into the car lot, they get caught by Mr. Big's henchmen, they escape from a savage jaguar, Chief Bogo tries to get her to resign early, and, eventually, they have to sneak into a secret compound guarded by timber wolves. Finally, for act two anyway, they escape the compound while they're locked in a containment unit with the timber wolves closing in.

Act two of *Zootopia* gives us a master class in taking one big goal that goes across the whole act and breaking it down into a series of challenges that both raise the stakes and provide our character with difficulties to overcome. And at the end of the act, Judy Hopps has found the missing Emmet in forty-eight hours, but not just that, she has found all fourteen missing predators. Which takes us into act three.

Act Three

At this point in the movie, it would seem that Judy Hopps has achieved all her goals. She cracked the case and is accepted as a police officer. She is even congratulated by the new mayor. But things haven't worked out how Judy imagined. Her investigation has created panic in Zootropolis, and she has lost her best friend in the city. She found the missing person, but Emmett Otterton isn't like he was before. He has "gone savage," as have the other missing predators. This creates a climate of fear as the prey animals feel like prey again and the predators are being persecuted. Judy gives up on her dream and goes back to the farm. She tried to be a good cop but "made life so much worse for so many innocent predators." Act three is about her finding out why the predators have gone savage.

Now, recall the two main functions of act three: this must be the most exciting and engaging part of the story and must provide a satisfying ending for the audience.

This has already been an exciting movie, so how do the writers of *Zootopia* increase the tension in act three? First, they take us into the assassin's lair. Now, this isn't an assassin in the traditional sense of the word; this is a family film after all. But we go into an underground laboratory in a graffiti-covered, disused subway station. Everything about this location makes it seem more sinister than where Judy has been before. Then we meet Doug, who is the chemist who makes the compound that turns the animals savage and we discover that he is also a sniper. What follows is a chase on a subway train that leads to the final confrontation with the true villain of the film, Bellwether, the new mayor. This is a conspiracy that goes all the way to the top.

In the final part of the conflict, Judy and Nick appear to be in real trouble. But they outwit Bellwether and manage to record her confession just in time for the police to turn up and arrest her. We could spend a whole chapter going over the ingenious ways that the writers of *Zootopia* used callback and payoff to set up this ending, but we don't want this to detract from how the three-act structure works within the movie. If you like analyzing the intricate details of story, then we recommend watching and rewatching *Zootopia*; there are very few animated features that are as well plotted.

In the end, Judy has exposed the conspirator. She has made up with her best friend Nick Wilde, and, what's more, he's become her partner on the force. Judy Hopps has become a great police officer and has made the city safer for everyone.

Overview

Whatever your tastes are in movies, it's hard to fault the structure of *Zootopia*. We have one overarching goal that goes from the beginning to the end of the movie—Judy Hopps wants to be a police officer. In order to attain that goal, we follow her through a series of three quite large goals. In the first act, we see her overcoming her physical limitations to become the first rabbit on the police force. But Chief Bogo doesn't take her seriously, so she is only a meter maid. In act two, she gets her first real case and must find a missing person in forty-eight hours. Then, in act three she sets out to find out why the predators are going savage. The story changes direction at each act break leading to Judy finally becoming a cop, but not just a cop, a great cop and one that is respected.

Three-Act Structure Case Study 2: Paw Patrol "Pups Go for The Gold"

Paw Patrol is a phenomenal success and is also a great example of a show that uses goals and the three-act structure. It charts the adventures of a young boy called Ryder and a team of rescue puppies. The show follows a format that involves a general introduction to the episode, culminating in a situation that requires a rescue (act one). Act two consists of the Paw Patrol team attempting the rescue, but then a new development occurs that increases the stakes and changes the rescue scenario, moving us into act three. The episodes finish with the rescue being complete.

That may be quite simplified but understanding and being able to analyze the "DNA" of a show is a powerful tool and will be covered later in Chapter 20. But let's see how that format plays out over the selected episode. This episode, "Pups Go for The Gold" is from season 5 of *Paw Patrol*.

Act One

We open on a prospector, called Uncle Otis, who discovers a huge gold nugget. In this opening scene, we also see his friendship with a beaver who helps him to uncover the nugget. While this friendship doesn't seem essential at the start of the episode, it does become relevant later. One of the functions of act one is to introduce all the main characters. Uncle Otis and the beaver are key to this episode, so they are both established in act one. There is also a scene that establishes the show's core cast. Ryder and the Paw Patrol puppies are playing a game as they try to find a rubber chew toy called Chewington.

These two scenes also help us to establish the world in which *Paw Patrol* takes place. This is a world inhabited by humans but it's also a world where the animals take on human-type characteristics. The Paw Patrol puppies talk and the beaver interacts with Uncle Otis as a friend, thumping his tail to a beat that Otis can dance to. The chew toy scene also makes it clear that while the Paw Patrol puppies talk like humans, they still play like puppies—another relevant part of the Paw Patrol world.

In the next scene, we learn that Uncle Otis is going to take the gold nugget into town because he has a surprise for his niece, who is the mayor. It's worth noting here that the niece is the only character in the episode that doesn't appear in act one, but she is still mentioned. But now a problem occurs. The mining cart that Otis takes into town derails on some old rickety rail tracks. We now know what the main problem will be for our characters—a runaway mining cart. Next, we are introduced to our final two characters, a pup called Everest and her hiker friend who are out bird watching. The hiker spots a "yellow-bellied-sap-sucker" and Everest spots the runaway cart, which she now calls in to Ryder.

Paw Patrol uses a "transition" device on the act break. This is a powerful tool in an episodic series and is especially popular in children's television. It makes the stories easier to follow, but also the kids love knowing it's coming and it gives a structure to the story that the audience recognize. When Ryder gets the call, he summons the Paw Patrol to the "Lookout," where the team suit up for rescue and get briefed on their mission. This is where the specific goal of act two is stated—to rescue Uncle Otis and stop the mine cart before it crashes.

With a show like *Paw Patrol*, which is essentially a team-based show, it can sometimes be tricky to pick out who the central character is. In *Paw Patrol*, it is usually Ryder. While the whole team is invested in the goal and each puppy involved in the rescue will have their own part to play, it is Ryder who is overseeing the whole rescue and coordinating the team.

We said that one of the challenges of act one is setting up all the information you need for the episode, while keeping it entertaining. This can be especially difficult in shorter forms that require all the information to be put across in only a few minutes. Look at how much information the writers of this episode have established in a very short period of time. Next, look at how they have used "mini-goals" to do that. First, Otis wants to find gold, then he wants to get it into town. The Paw Patrol team are trying to find Chewington. By setting up mini-goals and challenges for the characters in each scene, you can make act one engaging rather than a series of exposition scenes.

Act Two

The goal is now established. In Paw Patrol, the goal is always established very clearly as Ryder tells the team what their mission goal is during the transformation sequence.

In this episode, as the Paw Patrol team try to rescue Otis, the first thing they do is try to pull Otis to safety, but he doesn't want to leave his gold nugget behind in the cart. The first difficulty, Uncle Otis is uncooperative. But then, because of his hesitation, Otis gets whisked up into a tree and needs to be caught by Everest. The first part of the goal is now complete. Uncle Otis has been rescued but they still must stop the mining cart before it crashes, but now the mining cart is heading straight for Otis's cabin; there is something new at stake.

Now, look back at the previous paragraph and do a "but" count. In our summary of the second act, we have used the word "but" three times for a sequence that only lasts a few minutes of screen time. This can be a powerful tool in working out where your twists and turns are. If you're working on a story, count how many times you need to use the word "but" in your summary (the words "except," "unfortunately," and "then" are also helpful). Unless you're using those words to summarize, it's unlikely that you have enough obstacles in your story.

In the final stage of act two, Rubble, the builder puppy, builds a blockade to protect the cabin from being destroyed by the mine cart. Unfortunately, when the mine cart hits the blockade, the gold nugget is launched into the air. The nugget hits a tree and bounces back up the hill and starts rolling down chasing Everest and Otis. The first goal is complete, the mining cart has been stopped and Uncle Otis is rescued (at least from the first danger); the direction of the story has changed, so we move onto a new problem and the third act. The Paw Patrol team now need to stop the rolling golden nugget.

Act Three

The runaway nugget is rolling downhill chasing Everest and Otis, so now the stakes have changed as well. As Everest points out, the nugget could squish them. They need to get out of its way. Unfortunately, when they do, they see that the nugget is now heading toward the beaver family. These aren't just any random beavers; at least one of them is Uncle Otis's friend from the first act so the stake is personal. Next, and the final part of the emergency, Ryder calls in Marshall, the fire dog. Marshall uses his fire hoses to soak the ground in front of the beaver's dam turning it into mud. The nugget rolls and bounces toward the dam but sinks into the wet ground that Marshall has just soaked. The nugget has been stopped.

Ryder and the team help Otis take the gold nugget to his niece for her special surprise. He chips off a small piece of the nugget to make a gold pendant for her necklace. But this is a huge nugget, what is he going to do with the rest of it? Remember those "old rickety rail tracks" from act one? Uncle Otis wants to donate his gold nugget to repair the rail tracks. All the story strands are tied up neatly and quickly in the final scene. The Paw Patrol has saved the day and everyone lives happily ever after. For this episode at least.

Overview

Look back over the three acts of this episode, but think about the following things as you do:

1) Do a "but" count, but also include "except," "unfortunately" and "then." This was only a ten-minute episode of a preschool series, but look at how much actually happens. This is animation and in animation you want to move the story along quickly.
2) Go through act one and make a note of how the elements of the story are introduced in act one and how they each pay off in the rest of the episode. The gold nugget, beaver friend, the rickety rails, the Paw Patrol team, the niece, and the surprise.
3) If you can track down and watch the episode, time how long each act lasts. We mentioned that acts one and three will each last approximately a quarter of the episode time, while act two should last half the total length. In this case, those proportions are different. Paw Patrol sets up a lot in act one, so act one is longer. These are tools, not rules, and each show will have their own requirements.

Summary

In seeing how the three-act structure works, it would be easy to think that you can now write a story just by following the formula. In one respect you can, if you have a great idea but you can't seem to make it engaging, then applying the three-act structure to your idea will usually strengthen your story—there is a reason why this structure is so prevalent in film and television. But, this process does still require a lot of working and reworking to write a story that makes logical sense, fulfills the requirements of the structure, and remains fresh and exciting. If you're starting out, this will be tough at first, but the more you work with the three-act structure, the more it will become second nature and the stronger your story telling muscles will become.

Thinky Time #8

The next time you watch an animated movie or TV show, try to identify the following:

1. What are the act breaks? Is it a three-act structure?
2. What is the physical, "tickable" goal in the second act?
3. What are the obstacles the character must overcome to attain that goal?
4. Is there an act one and an act three goal as well?

Each show or movie has its own format. Most movies and TV shows have three acts but you may find that the animation you have chosen to analyze only has two acts, or maybe four acts. If so, look out for how the writers have used goals to drive each act.

Chapter 10

EMOTIONAL CONNECTION

We have discussed physical goals and their importance in driving the story. The next important ingredient in the story is emotion. Emotion gives us the reason why your character wants to achieve their goals, but it also gives us the reason the audience wants them to achieve those goals, and this is what makes a story successful. An audience doesn't watch a movie or TV show to see lots of action, although they might enjoy an action-packed genre; they watch to be engaged and experience a range of emotions with the characters on screen. Once you imbibe your character with emotion, it creates a connection that keeps the viewers watching.

When a viewer starts to watch a movie or TV show, there is an internal dialogue going on while they try to find their feet within the story. This isn't always going on at a conscious level, but they will be asking themselves questions like "who is this about?," "who do I like?," or "who do I dislike?" The earlier in your script that you answer these questions, the more the audience will engage with the characters on the screen and the more effective you are being as a storyteller. There is no one way to get the audience to engage with your characters, but there are six tools that can help.

You will see these tools used time and time again in animation; sometimes it will be just one or two of them, but often you will see all six used in the same story. It is important to note that most animation contains at least one of the first two.

Give Them Skills and Abilities

People have always loved a great story and some of our oldest known stories are the myths and legends. These were stories that captivated an audience who wanted to hear about incredible heroes, whether these were the Greek legends of Hercules and Achilles or the English stories of Beowulf and Robin Hood, America has the great Frontiersmen or heroes of the Wild West. Wherever you are, all cultures have great mythic heroes. What made these characters so fascinating to their audience? They were setting out to attain great goals, just like we covered in some of our previous chapters, but they also had incredible abilities and this has always held a fascination for the viewer, reader, or listener.

This is an especially important feature of animation, where exaggeration and fantasy are more easily accepted.

In many ancient cultures, the hero's skills were often strength or an ability as a warrior, but this could also include tricksters such as Hermes or Loki. These heroic characters dominate in the adventure and superhero genres. The characters in *Batman: Hush*, for instance, are only slightly removed from the gods and warriors of legend (see Figure 15).

These godlike characters have skills that will make an audience empathize with your characters today, but we can also look at much more diverse abilities to fascinate our audience. Tramp, in Disney's *Lady and the Tramp* lives off his wits using incredible street smarts as does Aladdin. Bart Simpson is a resourceful trickster, and we love characters like Speedy Gonzales and Road Runner because of their incredible speed.

Lightning McQueen in *Cars* is a perfect example of how a character's ability can make them attractive to an audience. When we first meet Lightning, he is not particularly likable, he is self-centered and arrogant and can't get on with his team, and he also doesn't want to be sponsored

Figure 15 *Batman: Hush*, August 6, 2019.

by Rust-eze because he wants something more glamorous. It would seem that there is no reason to like Lightning McQueen at all, but he is a great racer. We see his ability on the race track and we start to engage with him; in fact, he is so good at racing that we want to see more of him. His skill and ability gives us a good enough reason to follow him into the rest of the story.

Make Them Funny

This is almost the opposite of the previous point. A character who is good at everything is rarely funny. Occasionally, you get a quick-witted wisecracking character that can make the audience laugh, so their skills go hand in hand with their humor. Bugs Bunny from the *Looney Tunes* series is the classic archetype of this character, never outsmarted by Elmer Fudd or Yosemite Sam and never short of a good gag in the process. But usually, flaws are what makes a character funny. This is such a universal tool of comedy that you could almost draw a graph showing that the more inept a character is, the funnier they will become.

In the opening of *Minions*, we can see that the Minions themselves are not nice characters; in fact, they go looking for the most despicable individuals to follow. We can also see that they are not very skillful either; in fact, they end up killing everyone that they work for. They are however, very funny. Not because they have great one liners or a sarcastic wit, but because they are so sweetly stupid.

Bonus Material

Being skillful and being funny are not mutually exclusive qualities; a character can be both. In The Lego Batman *movie, Batman is Gotham's greatest superhero, but he is also self-centered, arrogant, and a terrible father to his adoptive teenage son. He is skillful in one area of his life, but not in others, and it is these character weaknesses that provide much of the comedy. Dracula in* Hotel Transylvania *has all the skills you would expect of the legendary vampire, but he struggles to exist in a world where the monsters try to live side by side with people, and, like Batman, he's not a good father. They both have some incredible abilities and some flaws and weaknesses.*

Whether it is Merida from *Brave* with her skill in archery or Bugs Bunny with his zappy wit and trickery, characters that are skillful or funny appear time and time again in animation. As always, there are exceptions to the rule. Sometimes you might want to create a story where the lead characters are not funny and have no exceptional skills and abilities. In these cases, the following four become even more essential.

Get Your Character on the Screen as Soon as Possible

The simplest way to get an audience to latch on to a character is to get them on the screen as quickly as possible and give them as much screen time as you can. Often, the central character will be the first character you see in a movie. If they are not the very first character you see, they may be the first character to speak, or maybe they are the first character whose face you see. Sometimes, an animation may open with a prologue that gives us some backstory or a scene with a villain, but we can normally tell that the characters in these scenes are not going to be the lead. Take the opening of *Ratatouille*. In the pre-credit sequence, we hear a voice-over and then the first character we see is Anton Ego, clearly a villainous character described in the script as "gaunt" and as having "fish-belly white skin." Anton is unlikely to be the character we follow in the rest of the movie. But then, who is the next character we see? Ratatouille himself, jumping out of the window nearly filling the screen. He even gets a FREEZE FRAME so the audience can take him all in. We know this is who we're going to follow for the rest of the movie.

Unwavering Resolve

In Chapter 4, we discussed how proactive the central character should be. Unwavering resolve takes this a step further. If we see that a character won't give up, no matter how many times they get knocked down, this is something that an audience is attracted to. Just watch Madame Souza in *The Triplets of Belleville* as she uses a paddle boat to follow her son's kidnappers across the Atlantic Ocean (Figure 16). One of the greatest examples of this character trait comes from Judy Hopps in *Zootopia* who goes as far as to state in her dialogue, "I don't know when to quit!"

Sometimes we do see characters give up on the pursuit of their goals at some point in a story, but it is important to highlight here that this moment usually comes a long way into the plot, after they've been

Figure 16 *The Triplets of Belleville*, August 29, 2003.

knocked down and bounced back quite a few times, and this moment often forms the end of act two.

A Little Niceness Goes a Long Way

Make your lead character nice in some way. It doesn't mean they have to be sickly sweet or an all-round nice guy or gal, but by giving your character some likable qualities, the audience will start to like them too. In the opening of *Hotel Transylvania 2*, Dracula is dancing with his daughter at her wedding and asks, "Is it everything you ever wanted, my little poison berry?" This is a vampire talking, but he cares about his daughter and wants her to be happy. Throughout the movie, we will see him put his grandson in danger and mislead his daughter, but this act of kindness near the opening shows that deep down he is worth caring about.

Any time we can see a character demonstrate kindness near the opening of the movie, it will engage your audience. Once the audience has connected to the character, then you can start to reveal more of their negative aspects. In *The Incredibles*, we see Mr. Incredible take time out from a car chase to help a little old lady get her cat down from a tree. Not long after this, he rejects Incrediboy and seems disconnected from his family, but the audience has already latched onto him emotionally so his negative behavior is more readily accepted.

Watch out for these acts of kindness. While not always present in a movie (Gru in *Despicable Me* is very sparse on the kindness front) that first act of kindness will help the audience engage with that character.

Jeopardy, Hardship, or Adversity

Giving your character hardships or adversity will immediately create sympathy for them. The audience will relate to them because they want to succeed and get out of the predicament they are in. In *An American Tail*, we know immediately that Fievel has a difficult life; he lives in poverty under permanent threat of being attacked by cats. Whatever happens later in the movie, we sympathize with him and want him to succeed.

Also, Fievel doesn't have this difficult life because he did something to deserve it, he was born into it. In *Rango*, the title character—a domesticated lizard—becomes lost in the desert after his terrarium falls out of his owner's car. The more undeserved these hardships are, the stronger the bond your audience will have with your character.

Bonus Material

When dealing with a well-known brand or franchise, some of these guidelines can be bent a little. If the audience is ready to watch Shrek the Third, *you can guess that a lot of them will have seen Shrek before and already like him. You will notice, though, that generally filmmakers don't take that risk. They will still employ some of these techniques in the sequels for anyone not familiar with the character and to strengthen the audience's bond.*

Chapter 11

THE EMOTIONAL GOAL

Now you understand how important a physical goal is to your story and you understand the necessity of having one central character. But what about that character's emotional journey? What about their happiness or overcoming emotional hurts that need healing? These character journeys are often an intrinsic part of an animated story but they are not as essential as the physical goal. Watch an episode of *Tom and Jerry*, *Scooby-Doo, Where Are You!*, *The Road Runner Show*, *Bugs Bunny*, or *Wacky Races*. Each episode of these classics contains a physical goal, but very little emotional journey.

Understanding and employing emotional goals within your stories is an important part of storytelling. While the physical goal gives us the "what" of the plot, the emotion gives us the "why." It tells us why the character is behaving in a certain way, and it gives us the biggest "why" of all—why we, as the audience, should care. In *Flushed Away*, we follow Rodney, a domesticated pet rat, who is flushed into the sewers and is desperately trying to get back home. Rodney's goal is to get back to his Kensington house and live in luxury again. But on this journey, Rodney sees what it's like to have friends and family and realizes that his domestic existence is lonely and that he would rather have friends and family than luxury. As a viewer, we can see that he's lonely and we want him to be happy, so we engage in the story and feel satisfied when he lives "happily ever after." Without this emotional healing, the "happily ever after" is missing.

While the physical goal is something that the character knows they want to achieve, the emotional goal in the story usually comes from something missing in the person's life. This is often something they don't know, or even believe, is missing until near the end of the story. Unlike the physical goal, it is not something that we can just tick off when achieved. Whereas a physical goal should be more specific than just "being happy," the emotional goal is usually about just that and is therefore much harder to define.

The character has the emotional need from the beginning of the story, and even though they don't necessarily know they have it, the audience probably does. Belle in *Beauty and the Beast* knows she wants more than her provincial life; in fact, she sings the words, "I want so much more than they've got planned."[1] But Rodney in *Flushed Away* has no idea that he's lonely; he's never known anything else. *Missing Link* gives us an even more complex emotional need. Lionel Frost, the lead character, can't make friends, but he thinks he can make up for this by becoming respected. Lionel thinks his emotional needs will be fulfilled if he is accepted into the Optimates Club, a fellowship for "Adventurers, Explorers and Great Men" but the viewer can see that the men in that fellowship aren't really that great. It will take the journey of the story for him to discover that all he needs is a true friend.

The emotional need often evolves out of a character's past. Sometimes this is stated clearly. In *Despicable Me*, we learn that Gru's mother always used to crush his dreams when he was a little boy. In *ParaNorman*, we can see that Norman is treated like a weirdo by others. In *Cars* though, we don't know why Lightning McQueen is as arrogant and self-centered as he is. Whatever the cause, the negative behavior that the central character demonstrates has, in some way, helped them in their life, at least up until the start of the movie or show that you are watching. In short, they feel they have no need to change it. This is the same with real people. If someone is a miser, then chances are they experienced poverty or scarcity as a child and now the hoarding of money gives them a feeling of security. It would be hard to convince someone with that background and character trait to suddenly start spending money freely.

It is often said that it's the journey not the destination that's important, but in an animated story the destination is just as essential as the steps that happen along the way. With an emotional goal, the character will be taking steps toward their character change throughout the story. But ultimately, the full change won't come until they reach their destination. In *Flushed Away*, Rodney doesn't know that he wants a family until he is back in his Kensington house. Lionel Frost doesn't know that all he needs is a friend until he sees how much he has hurt Link.

Although the character's emotional change at the end of the story may seem sudden, this can only happen if the right plot points have

1. "Belle (Reprise)" *Beauty and the Beast*. Walt Disney Pictures, 1991, Film. Howard Ashman & Alan Menken.

been threaded throughout the script. The emotional goal comes with complexities that we don't have when we plot out a physical goal. For a start, physical goals are normally clearly stated so the audience knows exactly where the character is heading. The emotional goal lies in the background of the story so the viewer will not be so consciously aware of it. The same is true for the character. For example, in *Frozen*, Anna's physical goal is to bring her sister back to Arendelle. By the end of the adventure, she will also learn what true love is, although she has no idea that she needs to learn this lesson as she pursues her physical goal.

If you are writing a movie, the character change is likely to be a big one. This is the way that the character has always been, so it will take lots of mini-lessons along the way to change the character's life. In a TV show these changes and life lessons are often smaller. When George in *Peppa Pig* is reluctant to go to the dentist, he learns pretty quickly that he will be okay. When Lionel in *Missing Link* abandons his dream of joining the Optimates Club, it takes a lot more to chip away at his life's ambition and teach him that all he needs is a friend.

Making the emotional goal work within a story is a fine balance. If there are too many life lessons on the character's journey, the story can seem moralistic and the character can seem dim and irritating for not understanding what he needs to do sooner. If there are too few lessons, the character change, when it happens, will not be convincing. Getting this balance right takes practice. Fortunately, there are four tools that can help with this plotting:

1. Defining the destination
2. Establishing where the character is emotionally at the beginning of the story
3. Creating the stepping-stones
4. Showing both new behavior and old, negative behavior

Let's look at each one of these separately.

Defining the Destination

When you set out on a journey, it's helpful to know where you are going. Once you have the core of your idea, think about what your character needs to learn, what healing needs to take place in their life, or what they need to change about themselves in order to be fulfilled. This won't normally be "tickable" like a physical goal would be, but like a physical goal it will be specific. Examples of this type of life lessons include to have friends (*Missing Link* and *Flushed Away*) and to think of others before yourself (*Cars*) or that beauty is found within (*Beauty and the Beast*). Once, as a writer, you know your specific destination, it is much easier to plot out the next steps.

Establishing Where the Character Is Emotionally at the Beginning of the Story

We know how the character is going to change at the end of the story, so now we have to think about their starting point. It might seem obvious, but this is normally the opposite of where they're going to end up. If your character is going to end up realizing they need friends, they must start the story thinking that they are perfectly fine being alone, and this must be played out near the beginning of the story so the audience can see the problem.

This is perfectly illustrated in the second scene of *Missing Link* when Lionel Frost demonstrates to his assistant, Mr. Lint (and to the audience at home), why he has no friends. In the first scene, Lionel Frost, in his attempts to photograph a mythical beast, puts Mr. Lint in a lot of danger. Now Mr. Lint is protesting.

```
                    MR LINT
          I'm a human being!

                    FROST
               (indifferent)
          One of over one and a half billion . . .

                    MR LINT
          It's no wonder you can't keep anyone
          around . . .

     Mr Lint exits, leaving Frost on his own.
```

We see clearly here that Frost doesn't care about other people and, as a result, is on his own.

Creating the Stepping-Stones

We now know our starting point, and we know where we're heading. All we need to do now is create little stepping-stones along the way to join up these two story points.

To do this, we need to think about what lessons the character needs to receive along the way. In *Flushed Away*, Rodney gets that glimpse of family life with Rita. This is something he seems to enjoy. In *Missing Link*, we see Frost have a real heart-to-heart with Link, and we can guess that this is the closest thing Frost's ever had to a friend. In these scenes, we can see where the characters are heading, but we also need to see them moving away from that destination. Our central character hasn't learnt their lesson yet, so they will still default to the old negative pattern that they had at the beginning of the story (at least until they are ready for the final big change). If a character started off selfish, she will still be selfish. If he started off obsessed with his looks, he will still be obsessed with his looks.

We don't like to mix our metaphors, but another way to think of this is to imagine weighing scales. Not the digital kind, but the kind that has weights on either side and tips back-and-forth to wherever the heaviest weight is. Now imagine a heavy weight on one side of scales. Now picture adding tiny weights to the other side, the scales will stay tipped toward the heavy weight for a long time. Eventually, enough of the tiny weights will outweigh the larger weight and it will tip over to the other side. Emotional healing in stories works in a similar way. A character's emotional need is like a very heavy weight that won't move easily. Gradually the life lessons and circumstances of the story build up until, at last, the scales tip and the character changes.

Showing Both New Behavior and Old, Negative Behavior

As the character moves forward in the story, these little weights will start to have an effect. The character will sometimes appear to be changing for the better, only to revert straight back to their original negative behavior. This emotional see-saw effect helps to make that final big change believable when it happens. These moments also work as a reminder for the audience; this is where they are going but they are not there yet. We feel a moment of happiness or relief when the character seems to be changing for the better, but then frustration when we realize that, of course, they haven't changed at all.

In *Despicable Me*, Gru has adopted three orphan girls as part of his plan to steal his shrink-ray back. By the end of the story, he loves the three girls but at the beginning he doesn't care about them at all, they are just a means to achieve his goal. As he pursues his physical goal, we see his new positive behavior starting to manifest itself but we also see him revert to his original, uncaring behavior. When one of the girls' toy unicorn gets disintegrated, Gru refuses to replace it, but then relents and sends out his minions to get one. It appears that Gru is starting to care, but later that night he refuses to read them a bedtime story and makes them all sleep in unexploded bombs. He leaves them by saying, "Good night, sleep tight, and don't let the bed bugs bite"—a moment of kindness? But then he finishes by saying, "because there are literally thousands of them . . . and there's probably something in your closet."

Summary

It is hard to think of a successful animated feature in recent years that does not contain an emotional goal. Likewise, it has become a big part of even some of the shortest animated TV shows. Much of children's television, for example, has evolved to include these life lessons. Emotional journeys are challenging to plot, but they are a worthwhile skill to develop as they are becoming an increasingly important part of animated storytelling.

Chapter 12

EMOTIONAL GOAL CASE STUDY

Shrek

As the theory of emotion in story is hard to grasp, it is best understood by seeing one in action. You don't need to see *Shrek* in order to follow this case study, but we still highly recommend that you watch it at some point. It's a great film and a perfect example of how an emotional goal works.

On the surface, *Shrek* is about an ogre who rescues a princess from a dragon and they end up falling in love. Alongside that traditional physical goal lies an elegantly plotted emotional story about a character who considers himself to be ugly and repugnant to others, but discovers along the way that if you give of yourself, and you're open about your feelings, you will be loved by others.

To analyze how the emotional learning works in *Shrek*, we need to go through the four steps outlined in the previous chapter, starting with how Shrek has changed by the end of the movie.

Because of his road trip with the endlessly positive, open, and upbeat Donkey, Shrek learns to talk freely about his feelings. He also learns to believe in and appreciate the meaning of true friendship. Most importantly, Shrek learns that true love can happen because he has fallen in love with the princess and she has fallen in love with him. The proof is that their kiss is indeed true love's first kiss, as it breaks her curse and turns her into the person she was supposed to be. An ogre like Shrek.

That's how Shrek ends up, as a positive, well-adjusted ogre. But how does he begin the story?

Shrek is a loner. He doesn't trust people. He is used to being shunned, ridiculed, and attacked by angry mobs. He is closed, guarded, and values his privacy, so much so that he puts a sign up outside his house with a scary face painted on it that reads "Beware Ogre." Shrek believes that he doesn't have a problem with the world, the world has a problem with him. This is the personality and habit pattern that Shrek has adopted and has served him well in the world up until now.

Bonus Material

At the beginning of the movie, Shrek is about as unlikable a character as you will find. So why do we like him as an audience? Why are we prepared to engage with him and follow him through the movie? If we go back to the six tools that create the emotional connection (Chapter 10), Shrek uses five of those tools, including both of the most important two.

Shrek has skills and abilities. In fact, he's practically a superhero. He can singlehandedly defeat a dozen soldiers and he's chosen by Farquaad to go and face the dragon. He's funny, he farts while he's bathing, makes candles out of his earwax, and has great comic delivery (there is a reason they use comic actors like Mike Myers to voice these characters). Shrek is also the first character on the screen and has unwavering resolve. Lastly, he suffers hardship and adversity—nobody likes ogres and we see an angry mob with torches and pitchforks coming to get him.

The only thing missing is that he just isn't nice. Maybe he's a tiny bit nice—he lets the mob run away instead of killing them—but he's not really. It doesn't matter, the other five tools are so well executed in Shrek *that the audience still like him.*

Notice how this description of Shrek at the beginning of the story is quite different to how he is at the end. The key storytelling point here is that he's not just different, he's opposite. Not opposite in every way, he hasn't changed from an ogre to a male underwear model, but the emotional aspects of his character have changed. Let's focus on that a bit more. Shrek hasn't made a complete change emotionally. He will remain coarse and probably a bit grumpy, he is an ogre after all, but the aspects of his character that relate to his emotional learn have changed. Shrek starts the movie as someone who is prepared to face a dragon rather than share his swamp with fairy tale creatures, but he finishes the movie as someone who is happy to party with those very same creatures. More importantly, he goes from someone who is guarded about his feelings to someone who risks ridicule by showing his love for Fiona in front of a church that is full of people. The film opens with Shrek wiping his butt on a story about true love's first kiss and closes with him delivering true love's first kiss to Fiona.

So how does Shrek make this miraculous change and, just as importantly, how does it occur on screen in a way that makes sense to an audience? Let's go through the three acts and look at the stepping-stones that bring about the character change. We will also look at the new positive behavior as it begins to manifest itself and how Shrek still reverts to his old negative behavior before the change really happens.

Act One

The main physical goal that we follow throughout the first act is that Shrek wants to get the fairy tale creatures off his land. So, he sets off to see Lord Farquaad to get him to give him his swamp back. But it's the emotional moments that run alongside this goal that contribute toward the character change at the end of the movie.

We have already established that Shrek, at the beginning of the movie, is a loner who likes his privacy. This is mainly because people are always running screaming from him and he is harangued by torch-wielding angry mobs. Then, he meets Donkey, and Donkey doesn't run away screaming. Donkey wants to be his friend. This is the first stepping-stone on his emotional journey. He has met someone who doesn't judge him just because he's an ogre. This already leads to a moment where, it would appear, Shrek is changing. Donkey asks if he can stay with Shrek. Shrek's immediate reaction is to say no, but when Donkey begs and pleads, Shrek wavers and says he can stay for one night only. It's a small change but at least he hasn't chased Donkey away. But then, the old Shrek rears his ogre-like head again and he tells Donkey to sleep outside.

Back at his swamp, Shrek is inside eating his beautifully laid-out slug n' slime dinner beside the roaring fire, while Donkey tries to get comfortable in the cold outside. Shrek clearly feels a little pang of remorse and is just about to invite Donkey in when he is interrupted by the arrival of three blind mice and a large gathering of fairy tale creatures. He tries to get them off his land but spokesman Pinocchio tells him that they were all evicted from their homes by Lord Farquaad and have nowhere to go. Eager to get back to his loner existence, Shrek vows to go and see Lord Farquaad and demand that he gets his swamp back. Notice that at this point in the story Shrek's desire to be on his own is so powerful that it drives the physical goals for both act one and act two.

When Shrek and Donkey arrive at Lord Farquaad's castle in Duloc, Lord Farquaad is about to start a tournament. The brave knight who wins this tournament will go and rescue a princess from a dragon (the princess that Farquaad wants to marry so he can be king). When

Lord Farquaad spots Shrek entering the arena, he changes the rules to
"Get the ogre!" A massive fight ensues and it's clear that, despite the
fact that they barely know each other, Shrek and Donkey make a good
team. Another stepping-stone for Shrek, who now has a friend and a
teammate, even if he doesn't want either of those things.

Farquaad sees how strong Shrek is and realizes that sending the ogre
to rescue the princess might be the best plan.

Act Two

The physical goal for act two has now been set. Farquaad will give Shrek
his swamp back if he rescues the princess from the dragon and brings
her to him.

Act two in *Shrek* is particularly interesting from an emotional
point of view. Often in animation, the physical goal is at the forefront
with the emotional journey going on in the background. In *Shrek*, the
emotional goal takes on an equal role to the physical goal. Look at how
the rescue from the dragon happens relatively quickly. Compare this to
Moana's journey to face Te Fiti or the buildup to Wallace and Gromit's
final showdown with Victor Quartermaine in *The Curse of the Were-
Rabbit*. The relatively quick rescue gives the writers plenty of time for
the relationship between Shrek and Fiona (as well as the relationship
between Shrek and Donkey) to develop.

Throughout the second act, the following stepping-stones all
contribute to Shrek's change of character during act three.

When Donkey reveals his misconceptions about ogres, including
the assumption that they grind down people's bones to make their
bread, Shrek starts to explain. Ogre's aren't as straightforward as
everyone assumes; they are like onions, they have lots of layers. This
is a big stepping-stone. Shrek might lose his temper at the end of this
conversation, but at least someone is trying to understand him and he
is trying to communicate his side of the story.

Soon the scary mountain comes into view with the castle on top.
The only way to get to the castle is by way of a very long rickety bridge
over boiling lava. Donkey is scared but Shrek tells him that he'll be right
there beside him and that they'll "just tackle this thing together, one
little baby step at a time." Shrek is giving his friend emotional support,
another indication of new positive behavior. Once on the bridge,
though, Shrek quickly reverts to type. Ignoring Donkey's pleas, Shrek
starts wobbling the bridge. He then "bumps" him backward across
it with his huge stomach. It's hard to tell if this action comes out of

friendship or irritation with Donkey, but when Donkey finds himself on the other side, he realizes that it's thanks to Shrek's bumping that he made it. Throughout this scene, we see Shrek's personality swing back-and-forth between new positive behavior and his older, ingrained response to events.

As we go into the rescue sequence, the physical goal for act two takes over. While there are some glimpses of the emotional aspects of the story during the rescue, Shrek, Donkey, and the rescued Princess Fiona are soon on their journey back to Duloc.

When Princess Fiona realizes that the sun is setting, she is eager to make camp. They stop and Fiona goes into a cave before the sun sets (for reasons we will find out later). Donkey and Shrek lay outside, looking up at the stars, and we get another insight into Shrek's softer side. Shrek tries to convince Donkey that the stars tell stories and the constellations are called things like Bloodnut the Flatulent but Donkey doesn't believe him. Then Shrek says, "Sometimes things are more than they appear." This is a tender moment between what would now seem to be good friends. It is a stepping-stone toward Shrek's character change and a moment of showing the positive behavior he is moving toward. But, as the scene plays out, we see Shrek's old behavior appear again.

Donkey, feeling more relaxed about their friendship, asks what they are going to do when they get back, and refers to "our" swamp. Shrek quickly reverts to his grumpy, old self and tells him that it's not "our" swamp "and the first thing *I'm* going to do is build a ten-foot wall around my land" and rolls over.

Donkey is hurt. They've been laughing and chatting and they have rescued the princess together and still Shrek goes back to this default behavior. "You cut me deep Shrek," says Donkey, and proceeds to give Shrek an accurate analysis of his character. He suggests that the "wall thing" is just a way to keep somebody out and asks him if he is trying to hide something. Donkey then adds with surprising emotional intelligence, "Who are you trying to keep out?" Shrek responds by shouting, "Everyone!" Then goes on to say that people judge him before they even know him and adds, "That's why I'm better off alone." The full scene is an important stage in Shrek's emotional healing, but as he still thinks he is better off alone; it is clear he has a long way to go. The wall he wants to build is real and the metaphorical emotional wall is still firmly in place.

As the journey continues, Shrek is clearly smitten by the princess. We have romantic music montage as the two spend time together. We see Fiona creating a type of candy floss out of a spider's web and flies for Shrek. She then inflates a frog and a snake to create two balloons that they carry together, like two love-struck teenagers at the fair.

Their journey is now nearly over. They are getting close to Duloc and the moment that Shrek will hand Fiona over to Farquaad. Shrek is feeling sad, but so is Fiona. As they eat together, Shrek asks if she would like to visit him in the swamp where she can try some more of his dishes. She tells him that she would like that and then just as they are about to kiss, Donkey pops up and mentions how romantic the sunset is. Fiona panics, it's that fear of the sunset again, and she rushes inside a nearby hut.

Donkey can see what is going on between them; he has "animal instincts" but Shrek is coyly protesting. Donkey tells Shrek to "wake up and smell the pheromones" and just go inside and tell Fiona how he feels. But the reality of the situation is dawning on Shrek. She is a princess and he is an ogre with no experience of love. As Shrek sets off sadly to collect firewood, Donkey goes inside the hut to find Fiona and tell her. It is then that Donkey discovers her secret. A witch's curse means that by day she's a "beautiful" princess, but when the sun goes down, she turns into an ogre.

Meanwhile, Shrek has made up his mind to tell Fiona how he feels. He is approaching the hut with a sunflower to give her when he overhears part of her conversation with Donkey. "Who could ever love a beast so hideous and ugly? Princess and ugly don't go together!" She is talking about herself, but Shrek thinks she is talking about him. He drops the sunflower. His hopes smashed. This time the stepping-stone moves Shrek away from his emotional destination, a device commonly used as we approach the third act.

The next day, Fiona, now transformed back into a princess, resolves to tell Shrek the truth about herself. But the previous night's events have now driven him back to being his old self, his emotional wall protecting him from further hurt. Shrek tells Fiona that he heard everything. Fiona assumes that Shrek knows her secret, so she thinks he hates her for being ugly. This almost Shakespearean misunderstanding means that they are now both hurt and angry with each other. Lord Farquaad arrives to claim his princess and proposes straight away. With a glance in Shrek's direction, she accepts. Shrek has the deeds to his swamp and the promise that the squatters have gone from his land. As he heads back to his swamp, Lord Farquaad and the princess ride away.

On the way back to the swamp, Donkey tries to tell Shrek the truth about Fiona; this makes Shrek jealous that Fiona and Donkey are pals, and he's soon angrily declaring that he is going to live alone in his swamp. This time he is shouting at Donkey and calling him a useless, pathetic, annoying talking donkey. Donkey sadly watches Shrek stomp off and it's time for a sad music montage. Shrek has achieved all his physical goals up to this point (although there will be a new one in act three), but emotionally Shrek is as far away as he can be from being happy. This is often an essential part of the emotional journey; a character only changes after they have hit rock bottom. Up till now they have been clinging on to their original behavior pattern, the one that served them well up until the story started, but now they realize how destructive it has been.

We just need the last few stepping-stones, or weights on the scale, to complete Shrek's character change. When the montage finishes, there is a sound outside Shrek's house. It's Donkey trying to build a wall. The two end up arguing and Donkey tells Shrek, "you are mean to me, you insult me and you don't appreciate anything I do! Always pushing me around or pushing me away!" Shrek asks him that if he treated him so badly, why did he come back? Donkey tells him that it's what friends do, they forgive each other. Another weight on the scale.

Despite this, Shrek feels hurt and his old behavior is in full swing. He tells Donkey that he forgives him "for stabbing me in the back." Then he storms into the outhouse—an echo of the beginning of the story—shutting him out. The final moments that create the character change comes in two separate statements from Donkey. First, he tells Shrek that he's shutting people out again just like he did to Fiona "and all she ever do [*sic*] was like you, maybe even love you." So now the truth is out there, Fiona likes or even loves Shrek. But Shrek's still angry, he heard her say that he was "ugly, a hideous creature." Now it's time for the final punch, Donkey tells Shrek that she wasn't talking about him, she was talking about someone else.

Shrek exits the toilet. All the weights are in place. All the stepping-stones have been crossed. Shrek realizes that someone might like him for who he is. This is a big moment, and it takes a little time for Shrek to shift to his new behavior. He apologizes to Donkey in an angry way. Then he finally softens and reaches out to Donkey apologizing with heart. The character change is complete.

Act Three

Shrek has changed now, but for the story to be complete, we need to see that change in action. We also need to see the beneficial results of that change. For that, we need the act three goal, the moment when the emotional story and the physical story come together to complete the journey. Shrek must stop the wedding and declare his love for Fiona.

Shrek arrives in Duloc but the wedding has begun. Shrek admits to Donkey that he loves Princess Fiona. This is the first time he has been this open about his feelings, and it shows how he has changed. But the biggest demonstration of this change is about to come.

Shrek bursts into the church to stop the wedding. He tells Fiona he wants to talk to her. She is resistant but Shrek perseveres. He tells her that Farquaad is not her true love. Farquaad realizes what is going on and taunts Shrek, asking what an ogre would know about true love? The congregation laugh; Shrek is being ridiculed again. The old Shrek would have run away and blocked everyone out, but Shrek is now prepared to show his feelings not just to Fiona but in front of everyone.

The emotional journey and the physical goals are now complete, there are just a few loose-ends to tie up. Lord Farquaad gets eaten by the dragon. Shrek breaks the witch's curse by giving Fiona her true love's kiss. He learns that she's an ogre too. Now they are ready to live happily ever after.

Shrek and Fiona marry at the swamp surrounded by singing, dancing fairy tale creatures, the very ones that he was trying to get rid of in the first act. He began the story as a loner and an outcast, closed and distrustful and with no friends. Now he has opened his heart, revealed his true self, and not only found a true friend in Donkey but he has also fallen in love.

Thinky Time #9

Choose a movie and complete your own case study of how the emotional goal works within that movie. If in doubt about what to choose, most Disney features from the last twenty years have strong, well-executed emotional stories. Then work through the following steps:

1. **Destination**. Watch the movie through once and then work out which character learns the emotional lesson in that story. Define what that emotional lesson is.
2. **Starting point**. Watch the first act of the movie again and see how the character starts their journey. What is the scene near the beginning of the movie that shows us how the character needs to change in order to be fulfilled? Are they aware of their emotional need, or are they oblivious?

3. **Stepping-stones.** Now watch the rest of the movie, and make notes on the scenes that point the character to the change that they need to make in their life. Also, note the times that the character still behaves in their original negative way.
4. **Examples of new and old behavior.** How many times in the story does the lead character appear to be making a change for the better? How do the writers demonstrate that the character hasn't changed yet?
5. **Testing the story.** Lastly, go through the stepping-stones that you have written down. Imagine taking out one of those stepping-stones. Would the story still work? What aspect of the emotional change is missing?

This five-step process is a good way to analyze a movie, but it can also work with your own scripts. If you're unsure whether the emotional through-line of your movie is working, just run through this five-step process. If when you reach step five, you feel that the story isn't working yet, go through the first four steps again. Have you clearly defined points one and two? Have you got too many, or too few of the stages covered in points three and four? Put these on a whiteboard or index cards so you can see them all in one place. Once you can see these all laid out clearly and in order, it is often simple to realize what stages you need to add or take away to make the story work.

Chapter 13

CHARACTER AND ARCHETYPE

You will have noticed that this book starts with plot and then moves on to character, so you would be forgiven for thinking that we believe that plot comes before character. The truth is that character and plot have a symbiotic relationship. Some writers are much more comfortable working out how characters are going to behave, whereas other writers prefer to think of great plot points and then manipulate the characters to behave in the way that suits their plot.

Wherever you start, character or plot, if you are going to write great animation, you are going to need to create strong characters. So, how do you set about creating these great animated characters?

Archetypes are our biggest power tool when it comes to putting together a cast of characters that are different to each other. For our purposes, character archetypes are models of typical characters that perform a particular function in drama and/or comedy. By putting archetypes in place, we can usually minimize the chances of characters performing the same function within the story—unless of course, you use the same archetype.

To really understand the value of archetypes, we need to go back in time—way before TV and film. Archetypes have existed since at least ancient Greece, but we only need to go back to sixteenth-century Italy and the days of *Commedia dell'Arte* (meaning "comedy by artisans") to see why they work so well.

Commedia Dell'Arte

Around this time, groups of actors across Europe made their living by traveling from town to town performing for the locals. Now, the likes of Shakespeare might have been churning out scripts in England at this time, but most of these acting troupes did not have a playwright among them, so most of what they did was improvised.

If you think turning up in a town and entertaining people without a script sounds like a scary way to make a living, you'd be right, but archetypes made these actors' lives easier. Over, certain character types evolved; this meant that an actor could take on one of the archetypes and they would know exactly how that character would behave. Whether they were the lusty old man or the dim-witted servant, each actor knew how to play their role. They also knew that none of the other characters were going to behave in the same way as they did and that the built-in conflicts that existed between the archetypes would help the drama and the comedy to develop. There were well over a dozen of these archetypes so there was always enough for each actor within the company to take one archetype each; that way everybody on stage would have their own priorities and viewpoint.

Entertainment has moved on since then and so have the archetypes. There was a lot of lust and lechery in those days. Today, we have archetypes in film and television that are as familiar to us as those older archetypes were then, and we can use these to help us to create characters for animation.

Archetypes Today

Below are some of the archetypes that we most commonly see in animation today. While it's not necessary to populate your story with every archetype, it is often helpful to avoid duplicating archetypes within your lineup of characters.

A Step Behind

As the name suggests, this character isn't too bright, but it doesn't mean that they're stupid. These are the characters who just know a bit less than the others; this can be through naivety or lack of intelligence but it can also be because they are new in some way. *Frozen's* Olaf isn't stupid; he's just been around for less time than the other characters and so understands less about the world. These characters usually have an innocence that gives them a puppy-like quality which endears them to others. Arthur Christmas (from the movie of the same name), Mater from *Cars*, and Butters from *South Park* are all examples of characters who are "a step behind."

Bonus Material

In children's television, this character archetype can be particularly useful as they can ask the questions that the younger members of the audience might want to ask. For example, in Peppa Pig, *George is the youngest of the main characters, which means that he'll ask questions about words or concepts that might be complicated for the younger viewers. This allows the younger audience to understand what's going on, without feeling alienated.*

Long-Suffering

The Long-Suffering character is often the one with common sense who can see the chaos that the other characters are causing. This is a character that can often be perceived as the "boring" one as they don't do the wacky things that we all love. But the Long-Suffering character is a vital part of the comedy as it gives us the audience's viewpoint. They are saying what we would probably say in that situation, but they can do nothing to turn the tide of madness around them. Lois in *Family Guy*, Marge in *The Simpsons*, and Spot in *Hong Kong Phooey* all fall under the category of Long-Suffering.

Dreamer

The Dreamer is one of the most recognizable comedic characters, perhaps because most of us can see part of ourself in that character. The Dreamer has ambitions and desires and believes that these dreams are attainable, although when they are a comedic character, usually they are not (the greater the ability the character has to achieve their goal, the less funny they are). Flint, in *Cloudy with a Chance of Meatballs*, demonstrates the Dreamer archetype perfectly. Flint dreams of being a great inventor, and when his inventions go wrong at the beginning, it's funny, but he becomes less comedic as his ability as an inventor improves.

Dreamers have a ton of ideas, a strong desire to achieve their goals, and a boundless energy to try and fulfill them, a combination that while funny can also be tragic. *South Park's* Cartman, Charlie Brown, and Jack Skellington in *The Nightmare Before Christmas* are all Dreamers, but so are more heroic characters like Belle in *Beauty and the Beast* and Rapunzel in *Tangled*.

Pompous or Arrogant

This one is self-explanatory. Whether it's a puffed-up academic, a superior liberal, or just someone who thinks they know it all. Brian from *Family Guy*, Squidward from *SpongeBob*, and Cogsworth from *Beauty and the Beast* are very different characters, but they all fulfill this role. These characters make us laugh again and again; they never learn their lesson, and everybody likes to see a pretentious gasbag brought down a peg or two.

Uptight

These are characters that range from being a little worried to having full-on anxiety-ridden disorders. The Uptight can be a bucket of nerves or a fastidious nitpick but we love to see them get wound up or wind others up with their controlling obsessions. Fear in *Inside Out*, Rex in *Toy Story*, and Tweak in *South Park* are great examples of the Uptight character.

One-Track Mind

This one sounds like it's all about sex—and it can be! *Quagmire* in Family Guy or even Louise in *Bob's Burgers* are both One-Track Mind characters focused on the opposite sex.

It might seem that such a sexual character would not have a function in children's content, but sexual drive can be replaced by other overwhelming desires. A character that thinks only with their stomach or has another overriding obsession can fulfill the same role. Scooby Doo's desire for food, Dug's (from *Up*) obsession with squirrels, and Mr. Krabs's (from *SpongeBob*) obsession with money would be child-friendly versions of the One-Track Mind.

Zanni

This character was so much part of *Commedia dell'Arte* that we felt it should keep its Commedia name. These were the madcap clowns of their day and where we get the word "zany" from—which should tell you a lot about this character. They were usually servants and can be singular but often appear as a group, causing mischief and chaos wherever they go. Lock, Shock, and Barrel from *The Nightmare Before Christmas*, the Werewolf Kids from *Hotel Transylvania*, and the Minions from *Despicable Me* are perfect examples of the Zanni in animation.

The Villain

While we all recognize the Villain, it is a complex archetype to understand. Sometimes the Villain is purely evil, characters such as the

Wicked Queen from *Snow White and the Seven Dwarfs* and the Joker from the *Batman* franchise have few redeeming characteristics. Other times, it can just be in the character's nature, Kaa in *The Jungle Book*, for example, just wants to eat something. Sometimes the Villain will have their own sympathetic backstory, so that eventually we understand why they behave the way they do; Gabby Gabby in *Toy Story 4* is one such Villain.

While the personalities of this archetype can vary—and will often be combined with one of the other archetypes to complete their personality—the Villain is the character that is most trying to stop your central character achieve their goal. While this might sound obvious, it is important that this character is in *direct opposition* to the central character. This means that the Villain wants either *exactly the same thing* as the central character or the *exact opposite* and not anything between or slightly different to these specific goals. You will save yourself a lot of headaches by getting this right in your story setup. But what do we mean by that? Let's look at some examples.

In *One Hundred and One Dalmatians*, Cruella De Vil wants the puppies dead, whereas Pongo and Perdita want them alive. These goals are in direct opposition. If Cruella De Vil merely wanted to injure the puppies, or borrow them, these goals are no longer opposite and will water down the plot. Pongo and Perdita wouldn't like what Cruella De Vil was planning, but the story when plotted out would not be strong enough.

In *Shrek*, both Shrek and Lord Farquaad want to marry Fiona. In this case, both characters want exactly the same thing. As only one character can be married to Fiona, these goals in are in direct opposition.

We highly recommend writing down the goals of your central character and Villain at the outset of plotting your movie or TV show. Make sure that these goals are in direct opposition before getting into too much detail. Time and time again, we have seen stories (sometimes by seasoned professionals) that have missed this point, or cheated them slightly, and they never quite work. It takes a lot of unraveling to change these goals once the story has been fleshed out.

Servants of Darkness

These are the characters that, while not the main Villain, will create obstacles for your central character to overcome. In many cases, these will be minions or henchmen of the main Villain of your story—Lotso's numerous hench-toys in *Toy Story 3* are this type of character. In other cases, these can be obstacle characters that we come across along the way. *Moana* gives us a perfect example of this type of Servant (and we see them introduced in the opening sequence of the movie). The Kakamora and Tamatoa both provide obstacles to Moana's quest, but aren't in the employ of any greater Villain.

The Trickster

As the name suggests, the Trickster is one of the trickier characters to categorize and understand. So, who is the Trickster? Loki, from the Norse myths, is one of the great Tricksters of legend (you can still see an incarnation of him today in the *Marvel Avengers* franchise). The Trickster is driven by mischief and trickery. As a lead character, he or she will often get their way by outwitting their opponents (Bugs Bunny), as a Villain they might ensnare people through a dishonest trap (King John in Disney's *Robin Hood*), or as a character that's just along for the ride they might just cause chaos for the sake of it (the Siamese Cats in *Lady and the Tramp*).

The Trickster is one of the dominant archetypes in myths, legends, and folktales of old, but it is still prevalent in animation today. Nick Wilde in *Zootopia*, Dick Dastardly, and Road Runner are all Tricksters, but so are The Riddler and The Joker in the *Batman* series and Prince Hans in *Frozen*.

Thinky Time #10

Choose a feature-length animation. When you watch it, try to see which character archetype best fits each of the main characters.

You will find that some characters can be quite hard to categorize. As the writers have fleshed out the personalities of their characters, they become more like living breathing people, but the archetypes are usually still there lurking below the surface. The more you do this exercise, the more powerful this tool becomes in your own hands.

It is also possible that a character is a mix of more than one archetype. Many Villains also have a One-Track Mind or could be Long-Suffering, a character could be both Uptight and Pompous, and some of the Servants of Darkness work as Zannis or are a Step Behind. By putting two archetypes together, you can create hundreds of character combinations

Chapter 14

ANTHROPOMORPHISM

When creating nonhuman characters for animation, there is a good chance that those characters will be anthropomorphic to some extent—in other words, they will have some kind of human characteristics. All the main characters in *Sausage Party*, Sven in *Frozen*, and even Daffy Duck all have human attributes.

Let's look at Lightning McQueen in *Cars* for a moment. He is a race car. He is powered by gasoline and needs his tires changed. But we also called him a "he." Lightning has a gender and he has a personality. He is arrogant, boastful, competitive, and confident. On one level, Lightning is a car but he also has some of the characteristics of a young boy.

Let us introduce you to a new word, although we're not going to use it as a word in its own right, we're going to use it as a suffix. The word is "-centric," and in this case we're going to add it to a noun to make a new word to help describe your nonhuman character. In the case of Lightning McQueen, he is a car so he will be "car-centric." Now that you know how this works, think of other animated characters that some of the following words could describe:

Toy-centric
Rabbit-centric
Gnome-centric
Snowman-centric
Vampire-centric

The "-centric" in this case refers to the aspects of your character that are not human. Gnomeo in *Gnomeo and Juliet* looks after the garden and freezes when there is a human about, that's his gnome-centric part, but he also falls in love with Juliet—just like his Shakespearian human counterpart. Dracula in the *Hotel Transylvania* series acts like an overprotective father (that's his human part) but he also drinks synthetic blood, has canine teeth, and can turn into a bat. He is vampire-centric;

fortunately, he is human enough not to devour a community, like Kurt Barlow in *Salem's Lot.*

Centric on a Sliding Scale or How Anthro Does your Character Morph? or The Goofy/Pluto Conundrum

While your nonhuman characters will have some human characteristics, it is important to define exactly how human (and nonhuman) your character is. What are the rules that surround the anthropomorphism in your show or film, or in fact for each character? These rules might not necessarily make logical sense—such is the wacky world of animation—but they should at least be consistent and you should be able to define them yourself.

Animation allows us to be outrageously illogical in ways that would be impossible in other forms of entertainment. Think of the fights that Peter Griffin has with the big chicken in *Family Guy* or nearly anything that happens in *Rick and Morty.* What about something as mainstream as the Disney Princess movies? In *Frozen,* we have a talking snowman who can push his own nose through to the other side of his head, and how does *Beauty and the Beast*'s Chip blow bubbles in his own tea? It doesn't matter; good animation allows us to suspend disbelief more than any other form of entertainment. What does matter is consistency. The more ridiculous the situation, the more important it is that you stay consistent. In animation, your audience will buy into nearly anything as long as your world and your characters obey consistent rules, no matter how ridiculous those rules may be.

Let us give you an example from the *Mickey Mouse* film series (pretty successful, right?). In these films we have two very famous dogs, Pluto and Goofy, and a very illogical piece of anthropomorphism. They are both dogs. Pluto behaves almost entirely like a pet dog would, and Goofy is also a dog but behaves pretty much like a human. To this date, neither of us have heard a small child refuse to watch the films because the rules don't make any sense. This is because their characterizations are both strong and consistent.

Now let's get back to the anthropomorphic sliding scale, and here Pluto and Goofy can help us again. If we were to lay out a scale of dog anthropomorphism in animation, we could put Pluto at one end and Goofy at the other—going from nearly fully dog to nearly fully human. Now, where would you put Nana in *Peter Pan* on that scale? What about Mutley or Huckleberry Hound? Depending on which aspects of their characters you focus on, you might put them in a different place. It would be hard, for example, to decide who is most doglike out of Scooby Doo and Gromit. Scooby Doo for the most part behaves like a dog, but he eats huge sandwiches and can kind of talk. Gromit on the other hand is almost human in many respects (he can even invent things), but he can't talk and many of the other characters treat him like a regular dog. In each case, their characterizations are consistent so the audience is never confused.

Bonus Material

If you want to see a meta-conversation where animation writers highlight their own logic (in what seems like an illogical setup), watch the Love, Blactually episode of Family Guy. *When Stewie and Brian go to visit Cleveland's wife, Loretta, they discuss the logic of which characters can understand Stewie based on his relationship to his immediate family.*

Making Your Anthropomorphism Relevant

Whenever you give a nonhuman character human traits, it is usually beneficial to make the nonhuman aspects of their character relevant in some way—no matter where they come on the sliding scale. It is rare that a nonhuman character behaves entirely like a human. Whatever the character is—machine, sausage, or horse—it will usually have some bearing on their behavior or physicality. If they are on the very human end of the scale, this aspect only needs to be tiny but it should still be relevant. Why make the characters in *Rango* desert creatures, if their creature behaviors are not going to have any bearing on the story? Where each of the characters are in the food chain impacts on the story all the way through (see Figure 17). The townsfolk are afraid of the rattlesnake character, but the rattlesnake is afraid of the hawk character—everyone is afraid of the hawk.

This is when you need to go back to that word "-centric" again. When you create an anthropomorphic character, it is important to know in what ways they behave like a human. But it's also important to give them that "-centric" skew. Think about Puss in Boots from the *Shrek* movies. He could easily have been a great sword fighter that displayed no catlike characteristics, but he is a cat and, therefore, he coughs up hairballs, chases lights, and gives us cute kitten looks. By taking a character that

Figure 17 *Rango*, March 4, 2011.

could have acted in an entirely human way and giving him the right catlike attributes, the writers have created one of the great animated characters—he even got his own spin-off movie.

Creative Variations

The kind of character hybrids we have been talking about aren't limited to anthropomorphism. A nonhuman character doesn't always need to have human traits; it could, for instance, have animal traits. Dino in *The Flintstones* is a dinosaur that behaves like a dog (there are no human aspects to his character). While most of the furniture in *Beauty and the Beast* has human qualities, the footstool acts like a dog. Or, for a completely different skew on anthropomorphism, look at *The Boss Baby*. Here, we have a baby who has attributes of an adult—a human combined with another type of human.

Animation provides us with never-ending ways to create character combinations. It is fascinating to see the new and creative ways that storytellers use anthropomorphism to invent new characters. We encourage you to do the same.

Chapter 15

PUTTING YOUR CHARACTER TOGETHER

Archetypes and anthropomorphism are great building blocks, but there are five more tools you can use to breathe life into your characters.

1. Physicality
2. History
3. Speech patterns, mannerisms, and catchphrases
4. Skills and ineptitudes
5. Likes and dislikes

Let's look at each one of these in turn.

Physicality

How big or small is your character? What about fast or slow? Strong or weak? If your character is anthropomorphic, this might influence your decisions. The sloth in *Zootopia* is very slow, as you might expect, but you could also go against expectations and create a bloodhound character with no sense of smell.

History

Where did your character grow up? Have they had jobs or been to school? Think of the Town Mouse and the Country Mouse from *Aesop's Fables*; they are both mice but their respective histories affect their outlook on life. When you look at your character's history, you are defining everything that the character has done up until we meet them on screen. In some cases, this history will become part of the story, but often it is just there to give the character an extra dimension.

Mr. Pricklepants in *Toy Story 3* considers himself to be an actor; we don't know what he's acted in before meeting him, but his acting past influences nearly every line of his dialogue.

Speech Patterns, Mannerisms, and Catchphrases

Your character's history may influence this. If your character grew up in The Bronx, then that will affect how they speak. But the character might also have a mannerism that is independent of their history. Watch how Bo Peep is always adjusting Woody's hat in *Toy Story 4*. Maybe your character has a catchphrase like "What's up, Doc?" Not every character has an individual speech pattern, a mannerism, and a catchphrase, but consider which ones might be effective as you write down your ideas.

Skills and Ineptitudes

What is your character good and bad at? Shrek is very strong but has no personal skills. Nick Wilde in *Zootopia* isn't strong but is quick thinking and devious. It is often tempting to leave out the ineptitudes, but a character that has both strengths and weaknesses is more realistic and engaging.

Likes and Dislikes

These can be big or small. Shrek's dislike of company sends him off to face a dragon. Captain Hook hates (and fears) the crocodile because it ate his hand. But these can be small things too. Wallace from the *Wallace and Gromit* films loves cheese, particularly Wensleydale. Ken in *Toy Story 3* likes clothes, and he doesn't like it when other people mess them up.

In each case, these tools are about asking yourself questions and then answering them. Be as specific as you can when answering these questions. Usually, when writing for animation the more specific you can be with your answers, the stronger your character will become. Beans in *Rango* isn't just a lizard, but she's specifically a desert iguana, whereas Rango himself is a chameleon.

Thinky Time #11

Put a complete character together. If you are working on a specific project that needs a character, then by all means use this exercise to develop the character you need. If not, use this like a blank canvas that might inspire a new story idea. We will assume that for this exercise your character will be anthropomorphic. Now go through the following steps:

1. What is your character? A robot, a bumble bee, a magic wand? What word are you going to put before "centric" when you describe them?
2. What main archetype do they fall under?
3. Are they a mix of two archetypes? If so, what's the second archetype?
4. Describe them physically.
5. Where were they born? What has their life been like up till the start of the story? What, if any, jobs have they done?
6. Give them a speech pattern (this could be a dialect or accent based on their history) or a mannerism.
7. Give them one thing that they are good at and one thing they are bad at.
8. Give them something that they like and something that they dislike.
9. Finally, if you haven't already, give them a name.

Once you have completed the process, try to think of five interesting scenarios that you could put this character in. These scenarios will reveal more about your characters as they come to life in your mind. You might find that these ideas form the basis of a two-minute short, or even a whole feature film. That's great if they do, but it's not essential. The main point of this exercise is to get you thinking about characters in a new and exciting way. (Note: if you need to create a human character, just miss out Stage 1.)

Chapter 16

COMEDY

If you're writing for animation, there's a good chance that at some point you are going to need to be funny. Much of animation is comedic. Some is primarily comedic such as the old *Looney Tunes* or more recently *BoJack Horseman* and *Family Guy*. But even some of the less comedic adventure films are filled with comedy. The *Frozen* movies, for example, focus on adventure but there is plenty of comic relief throughout the stories. Occasionally, you get an animation that has no comedy at all. The 2018 *Watership Down* miniseries, for example, was a dark political and social commentary with no room for comic relief, but these are few and far between in animation.

There's an old adage that says, "you can't teach comedy." We would disagree with that. Obviously, we all have our natural talents and some people are just funnier than others and we would agree that a funny instinct can't be taught, but comedy, like any other part of writing, has its own set of tools that you can use to improve the abilities you have. Most top comedians might look like they're just funny the whole time and are great to be around, but for most of them this is an ability they have crafted over a lifetime. Comedians analyze jokes, films, and other comedians; they try to work out what makes them funny and how they themselves can be funnier. Comedians make comedy look easy, but that's an illusion.

You might be able to guess then that there is a lot you can learn about comedy. There are volumes written on it, and you can spend a lifetime studying it. If you're planning on making a living writing animation, we would recommend you invest time in learning all about comedy and how it works. There are many writers who say that they don't need to, they are just funny, while that may be true, why not invest some time to become even funnier?

We imagine now that there is a question forming in your head. If there is so much you can learn about comedy, what can we teach you in such a small section of one book? An excellent question, because we can't teach you everything about comedy, but we can teach you what we feel is the most valuable and useful tool in comedy.

The Drop

"The drop" gives us the terminology that helps us to define the undefinable—what is funny about a moment, a scene, or a joke. It is not an exact science, but the more practiced you become at using "the drop," the more precisely you can apply it. So, how does it work?

There are three main categories that we can use to help us get better laughs in scripts. Often a drop will fit into more than one category, so use these definitions more as a guideline than a "law of comedy."

Drop in Expectation

A drop in expectation is the difference between what the viewer is expecting to happen and what actually happens. Let's take the sequence in the first *Kung Fu Panda* movie when Po is trying to get into the arena to see the Dragon Warrior being selected. At one point, he straps himself to a chair that is loaded with fireworks and intends to blast his way over the wall. The audience at this point knows something is going to go wrong, but they don't know what that thing is yet.

Po then gives us a big buildup. He lights the fuse as he declares that he loves Kung Fuuuuuuuuuu! But the fuse to the fireworks fizzle out. He hasn't gone anywhere. It's anticlimactic. Then the chair tips forward and he falls on his face. Most people were probably expecting this to have ended in a big explosion, with Po emerging from the smoke covered in soot. So, this is different from expectation. But the difference between what we expected to happen and what has happened isn't huge, so it's only a small drop and is only a little bit funny. What happens next turns this sequence into comedy gold.

Po is laying strapped to the chair, face down in the dirt. His father holds up Po's apron and suggests they get back to work. Po slowly starts to get up. The audience at this point expects that the comedy is over, only then do the fireworks ignite. Po is blasted along the ground face first into the wall. As he can't go forward, he is dragged, face first, back-and-forth along the wall. As if the indignity wasn't bad enough, the fireworks then blast him high into the air, hundreds of feet above the arena. Finally, the fireworks fizzle out leaving Po with nothing to keep him in the air, so he plummets down to the arena.

Figure 18 *Fast and Furry-ous*, September 1949.

In this scene, the audience probably expected that something was going to go wrong. They might have been thinking, "I bet those fireworks are just going to explode." The thing that made this funny is the difference between the expectation and what actually happened. The gap between that expectation and the reality is "the drop" in that scene.

A drop in expectation can also come from a character's reaction. An overreaction to a small event can be funny, but an underreaction to a big event will also give us a laugh. Wile E. Coyote is great at giving a long-suffering look to camera just before he plummets into a canyon (Figure 18), a serious understatement for the pain that is to follow. We can also get that drop in expectation by getting a different result from what we are expecting. When Wile E. Coyote hits the ground, he is never seriously injured in the same way that Po is not hurt by his escapades with the fireworks. In real life, the results would have been much different.

Drop in Status

A drop in status happens when a character's status is diminished in some way. We can see a great example of this in *Moana*. Throughout the film, Maui has been pretty sure of himself; there's no doubt about it. He thinks he's great! Maui and Moana go and retrieve his magical fishhook from Tamatoa, a giant monster crab. Their mission is a success, but when they end up on the beach, the magic from the fishhook has given Maui a shark's head. As Moana does her best to suppress a giggle, we can see that Maui is embarrassed by the situation and his status has been dropped. The sequence continues as the writers find new ways to humiliate Maui; he turns into a starfish, a fish, and a chicken. When he eventually seems to have his human form again, he falls over as he now has a fish tail instead of legs.

While the drop in status will work with nearly any character, it works particularly well with characters who see themselves as high status. This sequence of events would be funny if it happened to Moana, but it is particularly funny because it happens to Maui. Maui doesn't just think he has high status, he thinks he has the highest status out of all the characters so the drop in his dignity is greater.

This device is particularly successful when used on villains. Everyone enjoys seeing the bad guy's (or girl's) status being dropped. Nearly every funny thing that happens to Wile E. Coyote is funny because he is the villain and his status is lowered. Look at the terrible things that happen to Cruella de Vil and her henchmen Jasper and Horace. Jasper and Horace getting kicked in the rear by a horse does not have the invention of the *Kung Fu Panda* firework scene, but it's still funny because the audience love to see a villain's status being dropped.

Drop in Normality

The drop in normality is the difference between what we would consider "normal" and what *actually* happens. In the movie *Hotel Transylvania*, Dracula has opened a hotel for monsters. Much of the humor in the early part of this film comes from the difference between what would happen in a "normal" hotel and what happens in the monster hotel.

Most people have stayed in a hotel, so they know what is normal. They know what bellhops look like and how they behave, they also know about the signs that you hang outside your door that say, "do not disturb" or "clean up this room." *Hotel Transylvania* subverts this and gives us the monster version of these hotel norms. The bellhops are zombies whose arms fall off when they pick up the heavy cases, and those door signs are heads who actually shout out "do not disturb." We have a drop in normality by giving the hotel a monster twist.

Because of the ability to create fantastical worlds and images, this type of drop is probably used in animation more than any other form of entertainment. Whether it is the huge sandwiches that Scooby Doo eats, the stone-age twist everything gets in *The Flintstones*, or the car-centric world of *Cars*, we can see skewed normality throughout the whole world of animation.

How to Use the Drop

One of the scariest pieces of feedback you can ever get in writing is "this needs to be funnier." This note comes with a few variations, "not funny enough" or even just "funnier?" being two of them. Whatever the wording, one of the "powers that be" has read your script and decided that your witty line of dialogue or slapstick moment is not up to scratch.

Sometimes when you get this note, it is easy to address, and you just think of something funnier—problem solved. Often though, the solution is not so obvious. The note does not tell you why they don't think it's funny enough, and they rarely suggest something that will solve your problem for you. So how do you make the line funnier? This is where you apply the drop.

You now know that the drop is the difference between what represents the status quo and what actually happens within the scene. It's not scientific, so you can't measure it, but you can usually tell whether you are making a drop smaller or larger. We'll show you how, using that oldest of comedy devices—the banana skin.

Slipping on a Banana Skin

It's hard to tell why a banana skin is considered such a funny thing to slip on, but it is perfect to illustrate our purpose. Let's go into the scene:

```
Jim walks confidently down the street.

ANGLE a banana skin on the sidewalk, we can see
Jim walking straight towards it.

ON Jim's face as he <WHISTLES HAPPILY>

ANGLE the banana skin as Jim steps onto it.

ON Jim's face as alarm registers.

WIDE SHOT of Jim as he slides on the banana skin.
```

```
                         JIM
                 Wargghghghg!!!

   Jim <COLLIDES> with the wall and falls in a
   heap on the ground.
```

We have a small scene now that could be considered reasonably funny. Then we get that notorious note, "Can you make this funnier?" So how do we do that? This is a simple example so you might already have some ideas, but to use this as a diagnostic tool that you can apply anywhere, we need to understand the core of the gag. To do this, we ask some questions:

1. What type of drop is this?
2. Does this fall into more than one category of drop?
3. Who is being dropped in the scene?

Let's look at each question in turn.

What Type of Drop Is This?

We can't say that it's a drop in normality. If we see a banana skin on the floor in an animation, it would be normal for someone to slip on it. We would also expect it, so it's not a drop in expectation either. This just leaves a drop in status. Which it definitely is. Most people, if they walked down the road and slipped on a banana skin, would feel at least a little bit foolish, because their status has dropped. Now we know what kind of drop this is.

Does This Fall into More Than One Category of Drop?

From the aforementioned analysis, we can see that it doesn't. For the moment anyway, but we'll be coming back to that.

Who Is Being Dropped in the Scene?

In this scene there is only one character, Jim, so it's pretty easy to answer. You will find sometimes, though, that it takes some thought to work out who is being dropped. It can be more than one character, but usually one character is being dropped more than the others.

Now we understand the core of the joke. Jim is suffering a drop in status. So now we just need to make the joke funnier.

To make a joke funnier we increase the drop.

As this is a drop in status, one option is to make Jim's drop in status bigger. We need anything that will increase the indignity that he suffers. Status works two ways, so we can either increase Jim's status at the start of the scene or drop his status to lower as a result of him slipping on the banana skin.

What if at the beginning of that scene Jim has just announced that he is the greatest evil genius that has ever walked the planet. In fact, he is so great, he's going to change his name to Lord Jim Giant-Brain and everyone will bow to his great intellect. Now when he slips on the banana skin, his status has dropped more than when he was just plain old Jim. Next, imagine that at the end of the scene, he collides with the wall and falls backward into a big pile of dog poop. We could probably say that his status has dropped more now—it's hard to have high status when you're sitting in dog poop.

Let's just say that this scene is from a show that already exists and that Jim is a regular character in that show. We've entertained the idea that we could change him to Lord Jim Giant-Brain, but we can't change his character that much within the format of the show. We could look at other ways to increase his status. What if he's just told his boss where he can stick his job, and that he's his own man and is perfectly capable of going it alone? Pride comes before a fall and this might work within the show that Jim is in, particularly if the boss is watching.

We've increased the drop in status. But can we increase the drop even further? Let's look at the other way to increase the drop. Remember, there can be more than one type of drop happening at the same time.

The drop in normality is used a lot in animation, but can we apply it here? This is quite tricky as we're looking at a pretty normal situation—at least in comedy animation terms. The only way to make this a drop in normality would be to make it surreal in some way. Could the banana skin take on an anthropomorphic form, get up, and ask Jim how he would feel like if he got slipped on? We could maybe watch Jim desperately try to get up as a banana skin calls all his banana skin buddies over, and they all start slipping about on Jim as he desperately tries to get up and get away. This might suit some shows, but it would need to be appropriate to the world of that show. It might work in a cutaway sequence in *Family Guy* or in a strange dimension in *Rick and Morty* but is unlikely to fit into a more "realistic" world like we see in *Doc McStuffins*.

What about a drop in expectation? There could be a possibility here. Let's now imagine that Jim has slipped on the banana skin, he's hit the wall, and he's seen the pile of dog poop that he's heading toward. Jim

```
EXT. CITY STREET - DAY

JIM, a bank manager in a suit, struts down the street. He has
his head held high, <WHISTLING CONFIDENTLY>

                         JIM
                Who's the big guy in town? Me! I'm
                the big guy!

ANGLE a banana skin on the ground. In the background we can
see Jim's feet heading straight for it. His heel reaches the
banana skin and he starts to slide.

Jim's eyes widen as he <SHOOTS> across the pavement.

                         JIM (CONT'D)
                Waaaaaaa...

We go INTO SLOW MOTION as Jim looks down, his arms flailing
as he tries to keep balance...

ANGLE he's heading for a big pile of dog poop on the
pavement.

                         JIM (CONT'D)
                       (SLO MO voice)
                Waaaaaaaaaaa...

Jim has lost his balance and is falling... downwards towards
the dog poop... He is about to land in the dog poop when we
come OUT OF SLOW MOTION and...

<BOOM> a speeding car scoops Jim up, he bounces over the hood
of the car and onto the roof.

                         JIM (CONT'D)
                Help! I want to get off!

The speeding car <SWERVES> back onto the road and through the
traffic as a police car <SCREECHES> around the corner in hot
pursuit of the speeding car. <SIRENS WAILING>

Jim looks ahead, his eyes wide in horror.

JIM'S POV: he is heading towards a factory building, there is
a huge sign on the gate that reads 'GLUE'.

                         JIM (CONT'D)
                Nooooo!!!
```

Figure 19 *Jim and the Banana*. Script Sample.

is desperately flailing his arms around, his eyes wide with fear as he is doing everything he can not to fall into the doggy doo. We have now set up the expectation of where Jim is going to end up. Now we can subvert that expectation. Let's look at a revised version of that scene. It's on the script pages seen in Figure 19. Don't worry about the details of the script format yet; we'll be looking at these script pages again in Chapter 18.

EXT. GLUE FACTORY - DAY

We see a SIDE SHOT of the glue factory as the car smashes
into one side, closely followed by the police car. We hear
<CLATTERS & SCREAMS> before the car emerges from the other
side.

ANGLE the front of the Police Car with <SIRENS WAILING>. The
driver has mirror sunglasses and a determined look on his
face.

ON Jim still clinging to the roof, but now he is covered in
sticky, sloppy glue. Jim's eyes widen in horror again.

JIM'S POV: this time he's heading for a huge barn. The sign
over the barn door reads 'CLUCKY'S CHICKENS'.

EXT. CHICKEN BARN - DAY

We see a SIDE SHOT of the barn as the car enters one side,
followed by the police car. We hear <CLUCKS & SQUAWKS> from
inside. The car smashes out through the wooden wall in a
plume of feathers.

ON Jim clinging to the roof covered in feathers. He spits
some feathers out as the car races on. Then...

<BANG> the car hits a post and stops dead.

Jim <SOARS> through the air.

                         JIM
                   Waaaaaaaa!!!

EXT. PIG STY - DAY

A small group of pigs, slop around in the mud and the slurry.

<SPLOSH> Jim lands face first, in amongst the pigs.

Jim sits up, wipes the brown 'stuff' away from his eyes. He
gives a pained look into the camera, covered in glue,
feathers and muck.

                         JIM
               <SIGHS>

                                   DISSOLVE TO:

You've read it? Great! We're reasonably sure that most people weren't
expecting a car chase or a pig sty when they first saw the banana skin,
and, then, when he was about to fall, most members of the audience
were expecting a <SPLAT> into the dog mess. So, this is all a drop in
expectation. This new turn of events doesn't take away from the drop
in status; if anything, that might be bigger, but by adding the drop in
expectation we have increased the drop and created a bigger laugh.

When the Drop Is Too Much

Now that you understand how to adjust the drop, it is important to know that a drop can be too big as well as too small. If the drop is too small, then you end up with something that is not funny, or even worse, *nearly* funny. Nearly funny comes with an uncomfortable reaction as people want to laugh but feel like they're not quite getting it. We know how to make that drop bigger now. But if the drop is too large, you can get the equally uncomfortable reaction of people just being put off by your joke. If the drop is too big, the joke will be too tragic, too dark, or possibly considered sick.

To make things more complicated, the level of drop that can be tolerated will vary depending on people's tastes or the parameters of the show or movie for which you are writing. What might be a great drop in a show like *Rick and Morty* could have parents taking to social media to get your show banned if you use it in *Curious George*. Some people are fine with what might be called a "sick" joke, while others are more easily offended. You need to find a drop that is appropriate to the project you are working on.

For example, Figure 20 shows Kenny from *South Park* just after he has been killed in a game of dodgeball. In contrast, Figure 21 shows

Figure 20 *South Park*, "Conjoined Fetus Lady", June 3, 1998.

Figure 21 *Bunker Hill Bunny*, September 23, 1960.

Yosemite Sam just after he has been shot in the face with a cannonball. Yosemite Sam is surrounded by smoke but other than that he just looks a bit grumpy. He has been hit by a cannonball, whereas Kenny has been hit by a dodgeball and is a bloody, splattered mess in a way that you could never show in a children's program. In each case, the damage—and the drop—is appropriate to the audience.

Figure 21 also gives us a great example of all three types of drop being used at the same time. First, there is a drop in expectation; the image of Yosemite Sam when the smoke clears is difficult to predict. Second, there is a drop in status; Yosemite Sam is a high-status character, he thinks a lot of himself, so seeing him grumpy and covered in soot makes it harder for him to maintain his dignity. Lastly, it is also a drop in normality; it clearly isn't the normal type of damage you would expect from a cannon fire—we don't even know what happened to the cannonball.

Thinky Time #12

It's hard to improve on gags that have already made it to the screen as they have been written by seasoned writers and animated by some

of the best in the world. But you can still use existing animations to practice your ability to change the drop.
Either,

Choose a moment from a family animation that makes you laugh. Work out the core of the joke and then increase the drop until it becomes a darker joke that would only work for a grown-up audience.

Or,

Do the opposite. Choose a dark or twisted joke from an animation geared toward an adult audience. Work out the core of the joke and then decrease it to make it appropriate for a family audience.

Chapter 17

COMEDIC SITUATIONS

OR WHAT WE CAN LEARN FROM SITCOMS

So far, we have talked about how to increase (or decrease) the humor in an individual joke. Having said that, we would advise against attempting to add humor to a situation that just isn't funny—the comedy needs to be there in the first place. We see time and time again, writers trying to add a joke to a scene that they feel needs something to make it more interesting. This often involves someone falling over or the attempt to add one-liner-type gags by one of the characters. At best, these are painful to read; in the worst cases, they can just look desperate.

These problematic scenes that need "something extra" are the kind of problems that can give a writer a knot in their stomach. Fortunately, there is a solution. Unfortunately, it involves a bit more than just tacking on a physical or verbal gag. It involves reverse engineering the situation to make the comedy organic to the scene. Sometimes this involves a major story restructure, and other times it can just be a matter of tweaking the set up to the scene.

Some of the best comedy writers in the world are sitcom writers. A successful sitcom writer spends all day, every day thinking about comedy, comedic situations, and jokes. Sitcoms are also produced quickly compared to most movies and TV shows, so the writers get the feedback of seeing their writing on the screen quickly. But what can we learn from them?

A Situation Comedy is a Comedic Situation

Question: Why isn't *Friends* the best sitcom ever?

Answer: Because it isn't a sitcom. Not really, not in our opinion anyway. Well it sure looks like one. *Friends* fits into the regular twenty-two-minute time slot of a sitcom. It uses a few standard sets, like the two apartments and Central Perk. It even has the invisible character, Ugly Naked Guy, one of the standard motifs of a sitcom. And most importantly, it's really funny. *Friends* is one of the greatest comedy shows of all time, so why isn't it a sitcom? It might seem obvious once we say it, but the situation isn't inherently comedic.

The situation in *Friends* is a bunch of twenty-something friends, all trying to make it in the world. That's a pretty regular situation; it just happens to produce a lot of comedy. But *Friends* is the exception, rather than the norm, and that exception highlights what that norm is.

A comedic situation is usually a character or group of characters, struggling in a situation that is inappropriate for their personality, skills, or ability.

In *Friends*, the characters' skills are a "little bit" inappropriate for their situations, but not in a big way. Often their lack of skill is no more than a regular person in that situation—perhaps one of the reasons we can all relate to it. Let's look at some of the more "standard" sitcoms to see how those inappropriate skills work in various situations.

Frasier follows a psychiatrist who, while giving advice to others, is so neurotic that he struggles in his relationships with women, his father, and his brother.

Two and a Half Men follows a father and an uncle, who each struggle in different ways to bring up Jake. Alan, the father, is in an inappropriate situation because he is forced to stay with his brother who is a womanizer, a gambler, and a drunk. Charlie, the uncle, is in an inappropriate situation exactly because he is a womanizer, a gambler, and a drunk and he now has an impressionable child staying in his den of sin.

The Big Bang Theory, at least at the start, is about four guys and a girl. The guys are intelligent but with no common sense or street smarts. The girl who interacts with them is worldly wise, but has no idea how to deal with the geeks that have moved in across the hall from her. Leonard and Sheldon would be in an appropriate situation if they lived with other college professors, but they don't. Penny would be in an appropriate situation if the guys across the hall had six packs and liked to party, but Leonard and Sheldon haven't and they don't.

The most traditional sitcoms revolve around families. From *Leave it to Beaver* to *Modern Family*. We see this in animated sitcoms too. Look at *Bob's Burgers*, *Family Guy*, *King of the Hill*, or *The Simpsons*. In these sitcoms, the comedic situation isn't always obvious. These can look like regular situations to us, and one of the reasons the family sitcom is so successful is that we can all recognize and relate to the situation the characters are in. In each case, however, the characters are less equipped than most of us at dealing with the scenarios that arise. The parents can be too stupid, too awkward, too selfish, or too mean to deal with kids who are too stupid, too mischievous, too sexually active, or just downright bad.

Now that you see how the sitcom works, you will see that this setup isn't limited to twenty-two-minute episodic TV shows. We also see this in movies—especially animated movies. In *Ratatouille*, we see a rat trying to be a great French chef, in *Zootopia* we see a bunny trying to be a cop in a world half filled with predators, and in *Madagascar* we see zoo animals having to make it in a real jungle.

The model that we see in sitcoms exists right across animation. It's not always the lead characters with the inappropriate abilities. In *Road Runner*, it's Wile E. Coyote, who is outgunned in his situation, in *Top Cat* it's Officer Dibble, and in *Bugs Bunny* it's Elmer Fudd. It's almost like a mathematical formula; the less ability or skills that a character has, the funnier it becomes. Before you go and create a cast of completely idiotic characters (although that can work), let's look at how you can have skillful characters with inappropriate abilities.

In *Cars*, Lightning McQueen is a very capable character. In fact, he's a great racer, likely to win the Piston Cup. The problem is, while his arrogance makes him great out on the race track, it doesn't serve him well in a small humble town. Doc, the wise old car, has seen his kind before and is always one step ahead of him. Lightning might seem like he has all the abilities he could want but he can't escape the town of Radiator Springs until he has served his time.

The sitcom paradigm doesn't end there. The comedic situation doesn't just apply to the setup for a TV series or the premise of your movie. You can apply this to an individual scene or even a two-minute YouTube short.

Do you remember back in Chapter 15 we talked about giving your character "skills and ineptitudes"? This is when these can pay off. Sometimes you can have a character that is inept at pretty much everything, which can work well in purely comedic terms. *Mr Magoo* uses this exact premise; he can't see and so causes chaos everywhere he goes. Often though, we want to give characters abilities for the journey they are on, without giving them the skills they need in other areas of their life. In *LEGO Marvel Super Heroes: Maximum Overload*, Spiderman has all his spider powers that make him a great hero, but he suffers from teenage angst. Hiccup in *How to Train Your Dragon* is a talented blacksmith and can "talk to the dragons" but he is socially awkward as well as being skinny and weak compared to the other Vikings.

By engineering situations that your character isn't equipped for, you can make a scene that isn't funny, funny.

Bonus Material

It is important to note here that comedy is mostly about suffering of some kind. The characters that we are watching on the screen rarely know that they are involved in a joke. Comedic characters are often desperate or obsessed with something without the abilities to attain what they want in life. Occasionally, you get a wise cracking character that is always making jokes but these are the exception rather than the rule. Watch as Bugs Bunny gets out of life-threatening scrapes with ease, but also be aware of the suffering his opponents endure as he does so. Comedic suffering is usually subtle (if the suffering is too much, the situation moves from comic to tragic). In Hotel Transylvania, *for example, Dracula tries desperately to stop his daughter from falling in love with a human; this makes him more agitated than a tortured soul, but ultimately he is still not happy.*

Family in Sitcom

We mentioned earlier that family is the most common situation in sitcom. For every *Scrubs* or *Seinfeld*, there are dozens of shows like *The Middle*, *Black-ish*, *8 Simple Rules*, or *Fresh off the Boat*. This might seem like nonfamily sitcoms are a bit of an anomaly, but the reality is that family is often still present even when it is not so obvious. Let's look at *Scrubs* for a moment and imagine that there is a kind of pseudo-family there. What if we said that Dr. Cox functioned as a father, Nurse Carla a mother, and JD, Turk, and Elliot like their kids? In *Seinfeld*, if we think of Jerry and Elaine as pseudo-parents, when we watch their behavior on-screen, we can see that George and Kramer are the kids of the show.

Most sitcoms contain a kind of metaphoric family that the show revolves around. Even in *Friends*, the sitcom that's not a sitcom, Monica and Ross for the most part act like the parents while the other four are their errant children. If you want to look at how stereotypical the family is in *Friends*, Monica cooks and Ross is the character with a stable job—and just look at how difficult their metaphoric kids are!

When thinking about your cast, think about their familial roles within your setup. If your story involves a real family, this can be obvious, although you can still play against expectations. You could have immature and dysfunctional parents with children who are mature before their time. In this situation, the metaphorical roles might be switched. In *Rick and Morty*, Rick is Morty's grandfather but the relationship is more like one of older brother. So even though Beth is Rick's daughter in the show, her metaphorical role is as his mother.

If your setup doesn't involve family, can you use the metaphorical family in your cast relationships? The cast of *Scooby Doo* are a bunch of friends and their dog, but Daphne and Fred are like the mother and father with Velma being their bookish kid and Shaggy and Scooby their children that need a bit more guidance.

It is not necessary for the whole family to play lead parts in the story. In *ParaNorman*, the parents are in the movie, but take a back seat for most of act two. In *Wallace and Gromit*, there are only two primary characters. It might seem like the relationship is that of a dog and his owner, but Gromit is more like a long-suffering father doing his best to keep his adventurous child out of trouble.

Remember, each of the family roles can vary too. Children's personalities vary as do parents. A father, for example, might be a strict disciplinarian, but equally he could be a hapless dreamer instead, or what about a browbeaten and world-weary wraith? These are all stereotypes that if pushed too far will be obvious and corny, but using this tool can give you new insights into the relationship between your characters.

Thinky Time #13

Watch an animated TV show that isn't about a family. Try to identify the metaphorical family relationships in that show. Which one is the mother, the father, or the kids? Are all the family roles present or are some missing? If you dig deep enough, you might find some extended family. Is there a metaphorical grandparent in there?

Next time you watch an animated movie, look for these same family-type relationships. Remember, in animation the relationships are simple, so even the metaphorical family relationships are only just under the surface.

Chapter 18

THE SCRIPT

When we are writing a script, we are creating a story, that much is obvious. What we are also doing is completing a technical document that will be the guideline for lots of different departments that will be working on the story. When the script is delivered, it will go to the director, producer, and voice artists, but it will also go to the people who will be designing the sets and props, the people creating the sound effects, and, if it's a new show or movie, it will go to the character designers. Each department will be reading the script, but they will be focusing on the aspects that matter to them. Your script must be written in such a way that each department can easily access the information they require to do their job.

As a result of these script requirements, a system has evolved that is used on most animations. Today, scriptwriting applications complete most of the formatting automatically, and while these applications can be costly, they are worthwhile due to the amount of time saved when writing. When we were first writing, we were told that a script should always look like it was typed on a 1950s typewriter (the format did, after all, evolve from the old Hollywood studio system). It is interesting to note that despite the advances in technology, that still holds true. Most scripts are still delivered in Courier font—just like you get on classic typewriters.

Directing on the Page

We will now look at some of the fundamentals of formatting your script. While this section will cover the basics, you will find a comprehensive glossary of script terms in Appendix A. We recommend that you read through that glossary at least once so that you are aware of the range of script formatting techniques that are available.

When you write a screenplay, your primary job is to tell a great story, but you are also, to a lesser extent, a director. We can already hear various directors we know protesting. We can hear the words "don't tell us how to direct your script" echoing throughout the animation studios of the world, so we feel we need to clarify. The director is responsible for the entire visual look of the story. While you might be "directing on the page," there is a good chance that the director will overrule you and do their own thing—some might do it out of principle, but that's a whole other issue. For the most part, directors have spent a lot more time developing their visual sense of story than writers have, so we need to trust them. If you are a director, and you plan to write/direct, then obviously you can direct with as much detail as you like on the page. For the rest of us, what we need to do is portray the way you imagine the story being told. By including various camera angles and shots, you are showing one possible way that the story could be realized on the screen (and hopefully inspiring the reader to visualize your screenplay as they read).

Bonus Material

From our experience, there will always be a creative tension between writers and directors. Both are creative visionaries and it's unlikely that they will ever have exactly the same vision. If you allow this tension to build into conflict, this conflict might *affect the quality of the project, but it will* definitely *affect how much you enjoy the process. Our advice is to pick your battles. If you fight every single point, you will be known as someone who is difficult to work with. A simple home truth is that you are not right about everything. Get used to it. If you feel a story point is essential, explain your reservations about the direction the director wants to take things. The director has been brought in for their visual expertise, but you, as the writer, are there because of your story expertise. It is important that everyone is working toward the greater good of the project and that any creative tension makes it better.*

This next section refers to the two pages of script that you can see in Figure 19. We suggest reading through that now and then we'll look at the key points one at a time. You will have already read this script once in Chapter 16, but this time we'll be looking at the technical aspects of the script format rather than the story content.

The first thing you will see at the top of the page is the scene heading. These always start INT or EXT, meaning internal or external (inside or outside). This is followed by the location and DAY or NIGHT (occasionally there will be a variation such as SUNSET). Everyone now knows that we're starting a scene and where and when that scene will take place.

In the next paragraph, we have some stage direction (or action) that tells us what's going on in the scene and who is in it. In the layout of the script, we don't always give a camera angle or give the details of a shot, but we can still direct to a degree. Notice how separate shots are given their own paragraph. They are not always listed as shots, but the nature of the separate paragraphs means that we see them separately as we play the scene in our heads. Depending on the description, you might visualize a close-up, or a wider shot. You probably pictured the third paragraph, which says that "Jim's eyes widen," as a close-up, even though it doesn't mention a close-up in the description.

You will see that the first time Jim's name appears in the stage directions, it is in capital letters. This is usual in a movie script, and is there to make it easier to find the character's description (which should follow their first appearance), essential when trying to keep track of who is who in a movie with a large cast. This is not necessary for regular characters in an episodic TV format as everyone will already be familiar with the characters—although it might still be used if you are introducing a new character for that episode.

You will see that certain words or phrases appear in <POINTY BRACKETS>. These refer to visual and sound effects that need special emphasis. The sound team will put in the background sounds, for example the hum of traffic, if they feel like the scene needs it, but you should emphasize the various <CRASHES>, <BOOMS>, or <FLASHES> that are necessary for your story.

Next, you will see that the character and the dialogue are set inward from the other paragraphs. This makes it clear which parts of the script are stage directions and which parts involve the characters talking. Remember, animation is a visual form, so you will be aiming to have a lot more stage direction than dialogue. If you look at the third line of dialogue, you will see a set of parentheses between the character name and the dialogue itself. These parentheses are used to give direction on how the line of dialogue is to be delivered. These should be used rarely and cautiously. In the same way, we don't tell a director how to direct, we don't usually tell an actor how to act. We have added SLO MO as this will be a required audible effect, but it can be used to add words like "angry" or "whispered."

Lastly, you will see at the end of the script the words DISSOLVE TO. This is known as a transition and comes before a new scene heading (in this case, the new scene heading would be on the next page). So, why isn't there a transition before the other scene headings? CUT TO is the most commonly used transition; in fact, it is so commonly used that there is no need to type it between each heading. If there is no transition, a CUT TO is assumed.

One of the reasons for the standard script format is to get a rough idea of timing. When this was created for the movies, the guideline was that one page of script was equal to one minute of screen time. So, the script for a two-hour movie would be 120 pages. Animation tends to tell stories at a faster rate than live action, so this isn't universally true. We've worked on crazy, fast-paced shows where fifteen pages of script would equal ten minutes, as well as more sedate preschool shows that averaged around eleven pages for a ten-minute script. Script length will give you an approximation of film duration, but it's not an exact science and will vary from project to project.

That's the basics. Remember to check Appendix A for the comprehensive list of script terms.

Being Professional

It is important to get the technical aspect of writing your script right; it is also important to get the grammar and spelling right. These things might seem like pedantry but there are two reasons why these things are important.

First, you want to appear professional. There is an old story about the band Van Halen. They had it written into their contract that they demanded a bowl of M&M's backstage, but with all the brown candies removed. This for a long time was considered to be rock stars just being rock stars and seeing what they could get away with. When asked about this some years later, they gave a surprising reason for the demand.[1] It turns out, they had a very technical contract that was required for one of the biggest productions that had ever been on stage. They said that checking the candy bowl for brown M&M's was a very quick way to see if the venue had read the contract in detail. If the venue had missed that clause, what else had they missed? This is similar to a reader looking through your script for the first time. If a writer has got the format

---

1. Dave Lee Roth Interview "Brown M&M's," https://www.youtube.com/watch?v=_IxqdAgNJck

wrong, what else have they got wrong? Are they professional at all? How much do they know about screenwriting? You seriously do not want to draw attention to yourself by getting something as basic as the format of your script wrong.

Second, you want to keep the reader in the story. A script should draw the reader in, and get them to play the movie or episode in their head as they go through it. If a writer has done something as simple as put a full stop where there should be a question mark, or maybe put an apostrophe in the wrong place, it yanks the reader out of the story momentarily. They might stop and read back through the line thinking, "is that a question? Yeah, I think it is . . . . Okay, should have had a question mark." In that brief moment, the reader has come out of the story and you have an uphill struggle getting them to immerse themselves in your world again.

Now that you have a foundation in understanding the script format, we highly recommend reading as many existing scripts as you can. There are quite a few that are free to download online.

Chapter 19

DIALOGUE WORKSHOP

Live-action TV shows started with simple sets and one or two cameras. In the early days, camera technology meant that there was little variety in the shots and the restrictive sets kept movement to a minimum. These early technological limitations meant that the shows were dialogue heavy and more like theater than a movie. Nowadays, of course, we can go in for close-ups and swap scene settings more easily than in a play, but the dialogue-driven theatrical foundations are still there. Dialogue-driven scenes and stories are rare in animation. Although sound has been available for nearly 100 years, animation has its roots in the era of silent film.

The comedy duo Laurel and Hardy (seen in Figure 22) were one of the most successful acts to make the transition from silent films to talkies. There was a good reason for their success, they were comic geniuses. One aspect of that genius was how they adapted sound into their films. Sound when it came along was a novelty, so most filmmakers overused it creating movies that were dialogue heavy. Laurel and Hardy, however, added dialogue and sound effects where needed to complement the visual aspect of their silent films, without ever relying on the "talkie" aspect to tell their story. While both storytelling and technology have advanced, that principle is still important today. (Incidentally, you can still learn a lot about writing for animation by watching and studying Laurel and Hardy.) In animation, we want the dialogue to complement what we are seeing and not dominate the visuals.

Based on this, one of the first principles of dialogue in animation is that it should be brief. This is not the medium for long, unbroken monologues. Some scenes in animation might seem dialogue heavy, with a character saying a lot, but these "monologues" are normally broken up by action. And, if it's on the screen, it's on the page, so the dialogue will be broken up with descriptions of stage directions. This brevity might make dialogue in animation look simple, but to get to that perfect line of dialogue can take some time.

Figure 22 *Laurel and Hardy*, "Busy Bodies", October 7, 1933.

The Dialogue Exercises

Sometimes dialogue will just flow and come out perfectly as you type it. Sometimes it just doesn't seem to work at all. After a number of years of repairing and rewriting our dialogue, we have developed some tools to help when things just don't seem to work.

We will be coming back to brevity in dialogue, but for the moment we need to get writing. Dialogue is best worked on through practice rather than theory, so there are more exercises in this chapter than many of the others. We suggest you use this as a process. We have given you an example to work through, but if you're having trouble with a scene of your own, feel free to apply these steps to that scene instead. Often, you will approach dialogue with some of it already in your head, but sometimes you will just have a vague idea of what needs to be said or done within the scene. We often approach a scene by writing out the most basic, functional dialogue (as can be seen in Figure 23) and then refine and develop the scene using the tools in this chapter.

As we progress through the chapter, we are going to keep rewriting the same scene of dialogue. As we do each exercise, we'll be adding

```
EXT. CITY STREET - DAY

A large broken down DUMP TRUCK is parked in the street. BERT
and TINA, two tow trucks, <RUMBLE> into the street and pull
up next to it.

                          BERT
                This must be the dump truck we have
                to take to the repair shop.

                          TINA
                Must be.

                          BERT
                It looks very heavy. I'm not sure
                we've ever pulled a truck that
                heavy before. Do you think we can
                do it?

                          TINA
                I'm sure we can. We just need to
                think about it.

                          BERT
                I know, you hook up to the front
                and pull the truck. I'll get behind
                it and push.

                          TINA
                Good idea, Bert. Let's go!

Tina pulls up to the front of the dump truck. Her hook swings
out and attaches to the front of the dump truck.

Bert pulls up behind the dump truck ready to go.

                          TINA (CONT'D)
                Ready Bert?

                          BERT
                Ready Tina!

                          TINA
                One, two, three...

            BERT                          TINA (CONT'D)
    GO!                           GO!

Bert and Tina <REV> their engines as they push the dump truck
slowly out of shot.

                                        DISSOLVE TO:
```

Figure 23 *Boring Functional Dialogue.* Script Sample.

new things to make the dialogue more interesting and the scene will evolve as you go through the process. As the dialogue exercises create a sequence of tools that can be applied to a scene, we have given these their own identity and are not part of the "Thinky Time" exercises.

Dialogue Workshop # 1: Getting Down the Basics

In this first exercise, we want you to write a brief dialogue scene between two characters who are friends. We never want pointless chatter between characters so we're going to give them an objective. You can use something you already have in mind if you prefer, but, if not, let's just say that your characters are both tow trucks (Bert and Tina) and they have a particularly heavy dump truck that they plan to pull to the repair shop. These are friends and work colleagues, so they are not enemies and they plan to work together to achieve their goal.

We hope you write your own scene here, but to show how simple and functional the dialogue can be at this stage, please refer again to Figure 23.

Nice and simple. Nothing clever, but the dialogue is dull. The important thing is that we have a start. It's easier to change something that's not right than it is to create something perfect right off the bat.

Now, let's look at how we can improve it.

Objectives and Obstacles

In Chapters 2 and 3, we talked about the importance of objectives and obstacles. These are the essential building blocks of a story, but they can also be used in a more subtle way to bring your dialogue to life. In our tow truck scene, we have an objective (to get the dump truck to the repair shop) and we have an obstacle (a heavy dump truck), but what if we give our characters little micro-objectives?

Sometimes, these motivations can be an aspect of the character's personality that is always present. Scooby Doo is motivated by his appetite. In *Frozen*, Sven's love of carrots makes him try to eat Olaf's nose, giving an extra comic dimension to Olaf's introduction. Tina, in *Bob's Burgers*, is obsessed with boys, an aspect of her character that affects her behavior and her dialogue.

In other cases, it might be something that exists for just one scene. Near the beginning of *Hotel Transylvania* we see all the monsters check into the hotel. There is a lot going on in that scene; the main objective is for Dracula to greet all the guests as they arrive, but there is one set of mini-objectives that stands out in that scene. Murray, the mummy, arrives and clearly likes to be the life and soul of the party—he wants to be "the man!" Frankenstein, on the other hand, wants to bring Murray down a peg or two and uses his disembodied legs and butt to make it look as though Murray has farted. This isn't the core of the scene, and Frankenstein's desperation to bring Murray down is not a usual part of Frankenstein's character, but it gives us some great comedy and makes the scene more memorable.

Whenever you hear actors talking about their character's motivation, this is what they're referring to. It is not just the character's primary goal but also the things that influence the smaller details of the character's personality.

Dialogue Workshop # 2: Character Motivation

So, you have a new dialogue tool. First, you wrote a basic functional scene, with no pressure to make it good or interesting. Now, we want you to rewrite that scene but give your characters each a mini-objective or motivation that is separate from the main motivation of the scene. If you are working with the tow truck scene, what if Bert and Tina are freshly washed and the dump truck has just been filled with stinking trash? Neither of them want to be the one to be the truck that must push from behind as this will cover them in the dump truck's smell and dirt. What if Bert is getting old and is worried about breaking his drive shaft? What if they're brand new and still working out how to tow a truck?

Once you have given both Bert and Tina a character motivation, what if you give one to the dump truck too? Up till now he's been an inanimate truck. But what if he's afraid to go to the repair shop, like a kid frightened of the dentist?

Think of some character objectives that create conflict between the characters or extra obstacles for the characters and then rewrite the scene. It doesn't matter at this stage how long the scene goes on for; just have fun with it and allow as many ideas as possible to pour out onto the page.

The dialogue in your scene should be coming to life a bit more now. So, let's take it to the next level.

Character

We have now given our characters a motivation, next we need to know what they sound like. You may already have your character's voices in your head. This usually happens at a subconscious level when you hear the character as you type. This might mean that you have already started writing character-driven dialogue in the first stages of this chapter.

What we are going to do now is consciously increase how characterful the dialogue is. If you are writing for an existing show, this requires watching and listening to the characters over and over again, letting the voices, the speech patterns, and the attitudes of these characters become part of your thought process. If, however, these are characters you have created yourself, it's time to make some decisions.

There are three main areas that we can focus on to add life and personality to your characters:

1. **Status**. This doesn't necessarily mean official status like someone's the boss or a higher rank in the army (although it can). Each character in a scene has a *perceived* status relative to the other characters. One might always take the lead or feel like they're in charge. Sometimes this status is resented and sometimes it's accepted. In *Toy Story*, Woody has a higher status than the other toys, and everyone's fine with that. In *Moana*, Maui has a higher status than Moana and he's a pain!

   Status can function on lots of levels. You might have a high-status and a low-status character in the scene. Equally, you might have two high-status characters competing for top status. Bugs Bunny and Yosemite Sam are both high-status characters but Bugs always makes Yosemite look like a fool. Maybe you have a low-status character that brings down the status of high-status characters around him; going back to the silent era again, Charlie Chaplin's tramp character often played this part.

2. **Speech Patterns**. All characters, and real people for that matter, have some kind of speech pattern, and in animation this is often exaggerated. Occasionally, an animated movie will go for very naturalistic voices (see *Fantastic Mr Fox*), but usually they're more wacky than that.

   A bit like music, some writers have a better ear for speech patterns than others, but there are things everyone can look out for. Does the character have a catchphrase or even particular words they like to use? Think of "What's up Doc?" or "Yabba Dabba Doo" or "Beep Beep!" Is there an inflection or dialect that the character uses? Foghorn Leghorn is from the deep south and uses words and phrases that are quite different from Dracula, who is from Transylvania. If the character isn't human, does that affect how they speak? Donald Duck sounds kind of like a duck, whereas Yogi Bear doesn't sound anything like a bear.

   Look out for a rhythm, speech patterns, and inflections and try to include them in your dialogue. If you don't know what they sound like, it is often helpful to cast the character in your head. This is kind of like training wheels, a good way to get you going.

3. **Attitude**. Like real people, characters' attitudes will vary depending on circumstances. Any character (no matter what their base line personality might be) could be happy, frustrated, impatient, or

angry within a particular scene. What is the character's attitude, both normally and within the scene you are writing? Can that attitude be exaggerated? What is the reason for that attitude at that time? Can the attitude increase or change within the scene?

Dialogue Workshop # 3: Voice and Attitude

In the last workshop, you worked with the characters' motivation. Now we're going to take that scene and add a new layer, giving the characters more "character."

First, think about their status. What if we have it that Tina likes to think she's in charge and wants Bert to do as she says? What if Bert doesn't really want to do the job at all and won't listen? What if one of them lacks confidence? Or, they both think they're in charge. Maybe you could try giving them the personalities of Laurel and Hardy—they're both dumb but one thinks he's more intelligent than the other.

Once you have assigned some kind of status to the characters, it's time to think about a voice. Cast the characters in your head by assigning an actor or existing character to each part. What if Tina was voiced by Rebel Wilson and Bert was voiced by Josh Gad? How would this change if the voices were Sarah Silverman and Dwayne Johnson? These don't need to be the people who are actually going to play the parts; it's just a creative tool to give the characters vocal consistency. As you write more, they will soon start to take on a life of their own.

Next, give the characters an attitude within the scene. Maybe Tina is getting really impatient with Bert. What happens if Bert is anxious or the opposite, overconfident?

Once you have assigned status, voices, and attitudes to the characters, rewrite the scene again, breathing more life into the characters. At this stage, it is important not to edit down yet; that stage will come later. For the moment, just get as much personality as possible into the characters and the scene.

Bonus Material

Snow White and the Seven Dwarfs *might have been the first ever animated feature film, but we can still learn a lot about dialogue from watching it. We have in this movie seven very similar characters (see Figure 24). They're all miners, they're all approximately the same height, they all wear hats, and six of them have a beard. Despite these similarities,*

Figure 24 *Snow White and the Seven Dwarfs*, December 21, 1937.

each of the seven dwarfs has a unique and easily identifiable personality. In most cases, these are defined by their names but we also see it in their action and dialogue. Some of these characteristics are an attitude— Grumpy, Bashful, and Happy. Some, like Dopey, Sneezy, and Sleepy give us more of a physical manifestation of their characters. Doc, the unofficial leader of the team, is the only one that doesn't have a character attribute in his name. To dig a little further, we can also see status playing a major part in their relationships. Grumpy is clearly competing with Doc to be the leader, whereas innocent, naive Dopey has the lowest status of them all.

Action

At the beginning of this chapter, we spent some time telling you that animation was primarily a visual form and that, for the most part, dialogue should complement the action rather than dominate a scene. Since then, we have given you a series of exercises that have increased the amount of dialogue without adding to the visual elements in the scene. Now it's time to make your scene more visual.

In animation, even the most dialogue-heavy scenes tend to be interspersed with action. This action might be huge and dynamic and be the subject of the scene. In *Batman Hush*, Batman and Superman

Figure 25 *Kung Fu Panda*, June 6, 2008.

are having a conversation as they battle with each other (shown in Figure 15). Sometimes, especially in an exposition scene, the action might be more subtle. There is a scene in *Kung Fu Panda* that shows how subtle the action can be and still make the dialogue interesting.

The scene (Figure 25) shows Shifu (the red panda) talking to Oogway (the tortoise) in the opening act. There are thousands of candles lighting up the temple and Oogway is happy to blow them out one by one. Shifu, getting impatient, blows them all out at once. The candles provide a physical aspect to an otherwise dialogue-driven scene.

Bonus Material

For a masterclass on interspersing action with dialogue during exposition, watch the breakfast scene in the Oscar winning Wallace and Gromit: A Close Shave. *Any conversation set around a meal has the potential to be very static, but as you watch the scene play out, imagine the stage directions that would be necessary to describe the action in the script. Notice how many of the dialogue lines would be broken up by action. In addition, by making Gromit silent, all of his communication must be achieved visually. Remember though, a character doesn't have to be silent to give them lots of nonverbal communication. Body language and gestures go a long way.*

In our tow truck example, there is already something physical that Tina and Bert need to accomplish. If, however, we were to jump back in our story to the scene before, we might have a scene where Tina comes to get Bert and tell him the details of where the broken-down dump truck is. In its most simple form, other than Tina driving up and maybe pulling away at the end, this might be a scene with very little action. For a scene like this, in animation, we need to give the scene a visual element to make it more interesting (we're trying to avoid what we call "talking heads"). In this scene, we could add that Bert is being washed at the time and keeps getting water hosed over him as he tries to speak. Or, perhaps he is having his tires changed or an embarrassing oil leak repaired that he doesn't want Tina to see. These don't change the purpose of the scene, but they do make it more interesting to watch.

Whatever physical element you add to a scene, the action needs to break up, and be interspersed, throughout the dialogue. As a guideline, we try to avoid having more than three exchanges of dialogue without any action in between.

Some writers tend to imply some action at the top of the scene before the dialogue starts and assume that the director will fill in the action when they animate it. They might, for example, write that two characters are playing tennis, but then not describe the rally as it develops throughout the scene. This is lazy writing. If it's on the screen, it's on the page, and dialogue scenes should include the necessary stage directions, as well as any sound effects and "grunts" or "panting" in the dialogue that will bring the tennis in the scene to life.

Dialogue Workshop # 4: Keeping it Visual, Increasing the Action

Now it's time to rewrite that scene again, adding another layer of interest to the dialogue. In this pass, you will be filling out the action. You need to keep the characters active, constantly moving or doing something. This can involve driving around, trying to work out the best way to push the dump truck. Pushing or pulling the dump truck and not getting anywhere. Other lines of action could include a close-up of the tow truck hook attaching to the dump truck or a low-angle shot of the wheels as they start to roll. You might need to add extra dialogue to make sense of this. If you still haven't got enough action, you might need to add a new element to the scene, like an oil patch on the road that causes one of them to slip.

Once you've added the action, go through and make sure that it is peppered all the way through the scene. You should never have any long exchanges of dialogue without any action. Remember to add any sound effects or physical reactions in the dialogue as well. If one of the characters is revving their engine, that's a sound effect. If they are straining, a "Grrrrrr" or something similar needs to be included in that character's dialogue.

Lastly, go through the scene and see if any of the lines of dialogue can be replaced with a facial expression or a gesture. Silent communication can make a scene much more interesting.

Once you have finished, read it back. You should now have quite a dynamic scene—certainly one that's a lot better than when you started. But you're not quite there yet.

Making it Brief

You now have a scene with lots of ideas in. But, so far you've been generating ideas without editing and chances are there are bits you can cut out. Remember this is a dialogue workshop and dialogue in animation should be relatively brief. So now it's time to edit the scene down. This is your chance to make it dynamic and snappy.

The first and easiest edit to make is to take out any duplication. As you've been concentrating on generating ideas, it is highly likely that you have repeated your wording or, if not the exact wording, the meaning of the words. This is common and many writers do this intentionally to get the ideas flowing, but they need to be whittled away when you write the final version of your script.

Next, we need to take out anything that's not necessary to the scene. This might seem obvious, but to do this we must understand what those necessary elements are. It would be easy to look at this scene and say, "well, the only essential thing is that they get the dump truck moving." In this case, we could do the scene with no dialogue at all. Bert and Tina could turn up, one hooks up their hook and pulls while the other one pushes and off they go. If that's all that's required in your story, it would be possible to write that as a very short scene. But we want more from the scene than that.

When we write a scene, particularly one that is heavy on dialogue, we rarely just want to portray the most basic information. We might for example, want to establish more about the characters or the relationship between them. This could be anything from a physical aspect, to an attitude or maybe establishing their relative status. In *Kung Fu Panda*, when Shifu goes to see Oogway for the first time, we can see that although Shifu is higher status than the Furious Five (he's their teacher), Oogway has an even higher status than Shifu. We also learn that Oogway is old, wise, and more patient than Shifu and that they are old friends. On the surface, the audience is learning about the threat of Tai Lung, but they are also picking up aspects of character that would be missed if the scene was too short.

It can also be that a scene is there to provide information that is important to the plot. Scenes that just contain information are notoriously dull to watch, so the writer might want to add a comedic element to the scene to make it more entertaining. In which case, the parts of the scene that are necessary to the comedic aspect of the scene should be kept in (as well as the exposition that was the reason for the scene in the first place!). In the scene with Oogway and Shifu, the blowing out of the candles does not give us any information about Tai Lung, but it is essential to see the comedic aspect of Oogway's patience and Shifu's impatience.

Dialogue Workshop # 5: Making it Brief

We now want to boil our truck scene down to its essence.

1. Start by highlighting all the repeats you can find in the scene. You might like the rhythmical aspect of some of the repeats, but highlight them anyway. You're not going to delete them yet; you just need to be aware of them.
2. Next, work out what the real essence of the scene is. We know it's about towing the dump truck, but what else is it about? If it's about Tina being in charge and Bert being insubordinate, write that down. If it's about Bert being old and about to break down and Tina trying to look after him, write that down instead.
3. Once you have established the essential goals and character aspects of the scene, go through and cut out anything that does not contribute to those elements. Look out for long exchanges of dialogue with no action and cut those down as well.
4. Now, go through your highlighted repeats and delete whichever ones you want to get rid of. Be brutal!
5. Keep cutting until you have reduced your scene to two script pages.
6. If you haven't already, start reading your scene out loud. This might sound simple, but it is one of the most powerful tools when it comes to writing dialogue—after all, dialogue will ultimately be spoken.
7. Next, keep a copy of the two-page version of the scene, and then try to cut out another half a page. If you've done this, can you cut it any further?

8. Finally, read through your favorite version of the scene and check for typos.

Congratulations, you're done! What you should have now is a dynamic, zappy scene that is much better than you imagined it could be when you wrote the boring functional scene at the beginning. You also have a process that you can use to write great dialogue in even the most difficult scenes.

Summary

If you find that your dialogue is just writing itself, then go with the flow. These are great moments, and often your first instinct will be the right one. Sometimes, however, writing a good scene can be like pulling teeth. In those times, come back to this dialogue workshop and take the scene through the process we have outlined. You will notice that this process involves making the scene longer in the first exercises only to cut lots of your brilliant ideas out later. The temptation is to think it will save time if you edit as you go along. This nearly always stifles creativity and makes the scene less effective (and the process more difficult). The idea generation in the first four exercises is an important but separate process to the editing in the last exercise. To get the best results, you need to switch off the editor part of your brain while you're generating the ideas and then switch on your brutal script editor alter-ego once the ideas are on the page.

Chapter 20

WRITING FOR AN EXISTING SHOW

Ultimately, you may be aiming to create and write your own shows or maybe work in feature films, but most animation writers at some point in their careers will work on preexisting shows. It is a great way to hone your skill as a writer, earn a living (while you hone your skill as a writer), and get to know people in the business. It is also creatively rewarding. Whereas the principles in this book will equip you to write a movie, your own show, or an independent short, writing for an existing show requires an understanding of a format that already exists.

If this is a show you have been commissioned to work on, the production company will provide you with most of the information you need, but if you're planning on writing a spec script you will need to find out this information for yourself. Sometimes just being a fan of a show, or watching it over and over again, will help you to absorb that show's "DNA." It's possible to take in most of the information you need through this kind of repetitive viewing—especially when it comes to picking up the character voices and speech patterns. There is also a process that you can work through to analyze a show and understand it at a deeper level.

To do this, it is best to watch several episodes from a series and you will need to watch at least one of the episodes several times to complete this analysis. We suggest that the first time you watch it, you just enjoy the show and see how much you can pick up from that first viewing. What genre is the show? Who is it aimed at? Do the episodes stand alone or are there story elements that continue across the series?

At this stage, you should also think about why the show is animated. What are the fantasy and hyper-reality elements of the show? Is it just to do with the aesthetic and artistic style?

For example, *Rick and Morty* could (at least in theory) work as a live-action show, but the budget required for the various dimensions they

Figure 26 *Rick and Morty*, "Vindicators 3: The Return of Worldender", August 13, 2017.

travel to and creatures they meet would be massive. See Figure 26 for an example of a scene that would require a high budget in live action, but is standard in *Rick and Morty*. There is also an aesthetic element to *Rick and Morty*; how many actors would be able to deliver the same kind of comedy as the cartoon versions of the characters? This is a show that is animated not just because of the fantasy and hyper-reality, but also for aesthetic reasons.

Once you have watched your chosen episode once and you have a general idea about the show, a deeper analysis of the show can begin. Let's look at the various elements of the show you will need to understand.

Length

The first one is a simple one. How long is the show you're planning to write for? What you need is the length of the "body" of the show. The body is the viewed material that is specific to that episode. We don't count title music, end credits (if they're the same in each episode), or any ad breaks.

Next, check that all of the episodes are the same length. If the show is on network television, chances are the length will be pretty much the same for each episode (within a few seconds or so). If the show is online or on a streaming service, this may be less rigid so you may need to watch a few to work out the average.

Target Audience

Try to identify the show's target audience. In a show like *South Park* that's aimed at adults, you can estimate the target audience just from the show's humor, but things get more complicated when we look at children's programming.

A kid's show isn't just a kid's show. Each program will be carefully aimed at a specific age group and that age group might be more specific than you expect. A show might be grouped into the preschool bracket, or maybe the age group of five- to seven-year-olds, for marketing purposes, but the writing will actually be targeted toward a very specific "sweet spot." For example, Aardman's *Timmy Time, Jake and the Never Land Pirates* and *The Adventures of Paddington* are all preschool shows, but each is aimed at a different year within that narrow age range. Try running an internet search for TV shows aimed at three-year-olds, four-year-olds, and then five-year-olds, and you will find that the result of each search will be different.

Bonus Material

Whichever age group you are writing for, you will need to absorb and understand what is allowed and what is expected for that age group. Look out for what language can be used. In an animation for grown-ups the broadcaster and the time slot will dictate the level of profanity allowed. In a children's show, you will need to think about the complexity of language used. What about dangerous behavior? Preschool shows tend to avoid anything dangerous that a small child might copy, whereas a superhero show aimed at a slightly older age group will be packed full of danger.

It is impossible to outline every guideline for each age group, not least because this will vary by territory and broadcaster. It is also changing all the time. Now that you are aware of these elements, it will be easier to discern these factors when watching a show. Don't let the fear of getting things wrong tie you up in knots. You don't need to get it exactly right. People on the production team will give you feedback if you go outside what is expected for the audience. The key thing is to get the right tone to demonstrate that you understand the series.

Type of Animation

The main forms of animation used in film and television are currently 2D, CGI (3D), and stop-motion. There is a belief that the type of animation that the show or movie uses will have an impact on the writing. While this is true to some extent, animators in every medium are incredibly creative at reducing the limitations of their chosen medium. For example, in CGI it is much more expensive to create new characters and sets than 2D, where it is a lot cheaper. But in recent CGI shows that we have worked on, directors have redressed sets and shot the scenes from different angles to create the illusion of new sets even when we didn't have any. They've even given a character a "head transplant" so that a new character could make a guest appearance.

It is more important to use the guidelines given by the production company, or by watching and analyzing the show, than it is to limit your writing based on what you think the animation technology is capable of. The show's budget and the team's creativity will be the final decider, not the perceived limitations of the medium.

Plotlines

See Chapter 4 and specifically Thinky Time #6 on how to identify the plotlines in an episode. But this time, pay attention to which characters you are following in each plotline. If you watch several episodes, is it, for example, always the same character driving the A plot, but different characters driving the B plot? Do they change it from episode to episode? Do they always have the same number of plotlines?

Characters

The next task is to identify the core characters within the series. Look at the characters that the A and B plots focus on. Once you have watched an episode of a series a few times, you should be getting a good idea of the personalities of the core cast—how they behave and how they sound will start to be second nature to you. Also, check online to see if there are any fan wiki sites dedicated to the show. You can glean a surprising amount of information this way.

Bonus Material

Be aware of what outfits, clothes, or uniforms that the characters wear. Changing clothes in animation is not like changing clothes in real life. An actor can spend ten minutes in wardrobe and come out looking completely different. In animation, a change of clothes usually requires a considerable investment of time and money as it entails constructing and rendering a completely different model. This is much easier in 2D animation, but it is still rare to see many outfit changes in 2D shows. Movies like Toy Story 3 *might make the investment for the Barbie and Ken fashion show sequence, but most series won't be able to afford that. Try to avoid pitching ideas that require the characters to wear outfits that don't already exist.*

One tip that can be helpful is the use of hats or masks. If you really want a character to change appearance, it is much easier for the animators to add a hat or mask than to construct a full costume change. You might, for instance, be able to write a costume party episode just by using masks, hats, and accessories when the cost of full costume changes would have been prohibitive.

Most animated series start with a relatively small cast of core characters that will expand as stories and budget allow. In animation, due to the cost of designing and rendering, it is rare that new characters appear for just for one episode. The cost of creating characters will vary depending on the technology used in the show, 2D characters are much cheaper to create than a fully rendered CGI character, but no new character is free.

Bonus Material

This character information should give you a hint about a golden rule of writing a spec script for a show:

> *Do not introduce a new character unless guest characters are part of the show's format, or you have been specifically asked to do so—no matter how good you think your character or idea is!*

Breaking this rule, will single you out as a beginner. New writers often think that they have had such a great idea that the production company will be falling over themselves to include this character in the series. The reality is, it is unlikely they will have the budget to add that character and that the introduction of new characters will almost always be allocated to an experienced member of the writing team. Get the basics of the show right with the characters you have!

Act Structure

By now, you will be getting a handle on how the show you are watching works. You know the length, the number of plotlines that appear in each episode, the core cast, and the central characters. Now it's time to dig deeper. How does the act structure work in the episode?

First, separate out the different plotlines (see Chapter 4 for details). List the scenes for each one separately so that you can see each plotline in isolation. Sometimes, when the plotlines intersect, you may have a scene that contains important story beats from more than one plotline. In this case, you list that scene in each of the plotlines in which it occurs—so it may appear more than once in your act breakdown.

Once you have each plotline listed separately and broken down into scenes, you need to identify the following:

1. **How many acts does each plotline contain?** If necessary, please refer to Chapter 5 to help with identifying the act breaks.
2. **How soon are the goals stated?** Do the characters state their goals clearly, or are they just implied? How soon do we know what the big goal for the episode will be? This is particularly important for the A plot.
3. **Is the goal in the B plot (or C plot) as clear as the goal in the A plot?** Depending on how much screen time the A plot takes, the subplots may have goals of their own. If the smaller plots have only a minimal amount of screen time, they may be very simple and just be a running joke.

Now you really have a clear idea of how this show is working. Just two more things to go.

Sets

You may not have noticed this, but the show you are watching probably has a limited number of sets. Like characters, sets are expensive to build (even if they are only being drawn or constructed inside a computer). Most shows will have several core sets that are used—in the same way that a sitcom does—but there will be additional sets. Make a note of any common locations, but also generic sets such as woodland or city streets.

The production company is generally trying to make the world look as rich and varied as they possibly can with the budget they have. Your job here is to see through that. Notice, is it always the same street (or park or forest) when the characters are outside? If there are regular new locations, how many are allowed within the show? Shows like *Adventure Time* tend to have lots of new locations (it also has a simple style of animation), whereas *Doc McStuffins* has fewer.

Bonus Material

When you do this type of analysis, it's important that you view the most recent episodes available. This is especially true of a long-running series, as the cast of characters and the locations available will be different from the earlier series. The later episodes will also give you an idea as to how the series has evolved. Often, the themes and, more importantly, the relationships between the characters will have changed since the first series. There is usually a budget for a show to expand a little each season so the locations and the characters increase as time goes on.

Set Pieces

A set piece refers to a section of the show that happens in every episode and is part of the show's format. While these occasionally feature in live-action programs, they are much more common in animation—and you see them most of all in children's television.

There are three main types of set piece:

1) **Transformation Sequences**. A moment when the characters change in some way. Examples of these would include the pups getting ready for the rescue in *Paw Patrol* or a superhero getting ready for action—like Ben 10 transforming into an alien creature (see Figure 27).
2) **Song**. A regular musical interlude within the show. A set piece song does not include the theme song or a unique musical episode, but is a regular part of the show's format. This can be the same song each time or a different song in each episode.
3) **Montage**. While many shows might use montages occasionally, some shows feature a montage in every episode. A montage is usually there to compress time, but can just be visually entertaining or comedic.

Are there any set pieces in the show you are analyzing? If so, is it the same in each episode or does it vary each time? Is it always in the same

Figure 27 *Ben 10*, "Escape from Aggregor", December 27, 2005.

place in the story or does that change? Become familiar with the way the show you are working on uses set pieces; it will stand out if you use one incorrectly.

How Important Is This Information?

Essential. Going through the process of analyzing a show, using the aforementioned tools, will give you all the information you need to write an episode of any animated show.

This exercise also has another advantage. The more you do it, the more you see how shows and stories work—as we said, writing on an existing show is a good way to hone your craft. If you do this with several episodes of the same show, you will see how the plots and subplots interact with each other and you will develop a sense for how goals work to create story. The more you understand how successful shows work, the more likely it is that you will be able to create your own.

We highly recommend that you try out this exercise on your favorite show. We say choose your favorite show as you will need to watch some episodes several times, and it's more fun if you like the show. You will also have a deeper understanding of how a show you love works. But before you do, read through the case study in the next chapter to see the process in action.

Chapter 21

WRITING FOR AN EXISTING SHOW CASE STUDY

Bob's Burgers

The Premise of the Show

Bob's Burgers is an animated sitcom that revolves around Bob, his family, and his burger restaurant, which barely makes enough money to stay in business. Although the food is good, the problem lies with Bob's lack of talent when it comes to promoting his business, plus his family's wacky activities that often cause his plans to fail.

Length

A typical *Bob's Burgers* episode is around twenty to twenty-two minutes long including opening and closing credits. The opening credit sequence is fifteen seconds long and the remainder of the credits appear over the beginning of the first scene. Most scenes are short—around a minute long.

Animation Style

Bob's Burgers is created in 2D. The characters are simply drawn and rendered, but the faces are expressive. The team of talented voice artists bring the characters to life. Tina and Linda are voiced by men, which gives them an unusual delivery.

Why Is This Show Animated and Not Live Action?

In the case of *Bob's Burgers*, the answer is not obvious. There are no complicated fantasy sequences (like you get in *Family Guy*) or epic and expensive crowd scenes. The look of the show, especially the characters, is the main reason for *Bob's Burgers* being an animated show. They have a comic strip quality to them that would be lost in a live-action format. There is also the comedy which derives from the deadpan delivery of the three children who are voiced by adults. If this was a live-action show, the parts would be played by actual children, and the comic delivery and range of edgy and inappropriate lines could prove difficult if using younger actors.

Plotlines

Bob's Burgers usually has two plotlines (an A and a B plot), but occasionally uses a small C plot. Anyone writing a first script for the series should probably stick to the basic A and B plot structure.

Identifying the Main Protagonists of the Series

Bob and his family.

Bob Belcher (Male, 46) He is well-meaning, sensible with a sunny perspective but is always struggling to make ends meet. He is patient and kind but will lose his temper if anyone demeans or harasses him, chiefly Jimmy Pesto, owner of the nearby Jimmy Pesto's Pizzas. Bob receives little respect from his children but remains a hardworking family man who will do anything to make them happy.

Linda Belcher (Female, 45) Linda is Bob's wife. She is enthusiastic and supports her husband ferociously in whatever he does. She is flamboyant and extrovert, talkative, and loves theater. Bob and Linda have a happy marriage. Although Linda does have a tough side, she has been known to head butt turkeys and chase someone down if they beat her daughter in laser tag.

Louise Belcher (Female, 9) Louise always wears bunny ears, which could trick you into thinking she is sweet and innocent. In fact, Louise is aloof, cunning, and a bit of a trickster. She has a dark sense of humor and loves to create chaos. For example in the episode *Human Flesh* she started the rumor that Bob's Burgers contained human flesh. But despite all this, she does have a heart of gold. She is a fan of Japanese culture and loves her Kuchi Kopi night light.

Gene Belcher (Male, 11) Gene is the middle child, and is Bob and Linda's only boy. He loves music, can play countless instruments, and has written musicals. He is highly creative but has a short attention span and a gross sense of humor (his jokes normally revolving around bodily functions or his genitals). He can also be brutally honest with his family and doesn't feel bad when they get hurt.

Tina Belcher (Female, 13) Tina is a hopeless romantic who is obsessed with boys, which is unfortunate since she has terrible social skills (a good comedic combination). Although she is obsessed with sex, this is mostly age appropriate, and the show does not rely on shock for its humor. Despite her intense interest in sex, she still loves horses and rainbows, so while she is moving into her teenage years, she hasn't fully let go of her childhood. She also has a strong conscience and is often driven by guilt if she feels that she has done something wrong.

The Supporting Cast

The creative team have surrounded the Belchers with countless rich and colorful characters. There's regular customer Teddy, a bumbling handyman, known for telling long-winded stories and invading Bob's personal space. Linda's emotionally unstable sister Gayle. Health Inspector Hugo, an ex-boyfriend of Linda's who takes his job very seriously and is always trying to get the restaurant shut down. Jimmy Pesto, Bob's archrival and owner of Jimmy Pesto's Pizzeria and his son Jimmy Jr., who just wants to dance.

The Locations and Sets

Because *Bob's Burgers* is a 2D animation, the sets are quite simply rendered. The actual Bob's Burgers Restaurant is usually the central location but there are lots of sets available. Also, because of the nature of 2D animation and the animation style of the show, creating new locations would not be that difficult and story choices shouldn't be limited because they need an unusual location.

Set Pieces

Bob's Burgers uses five different set pieces.

1 Episode Titles Bob's Burgers titles quite often pay homage to movie titles, songs, or well-known phrases with a slight twist. The episode we will be looking at shortly is called "The Ring (But Not Scary)"; other examples include the following:

Legends of the Mall
Pig Trouble in Little Tina
Motor She Boat
Live and Let Fly
The Unbearable Likeness of Gene

2 *The Opening Credits: The Store Next Door* The opening credits always depicts Bob's Burgers and the stores that are either side of it. We then see a FAST FORWARD MONTAGE that shows the history of Bob's Burgers' various catastrophic reopenings, via fallen banners and pest control vans.

As this montage plays, we see that on one side of Bob's Burgers is a Funeral Home called "It's Your Funeral Home & Crematorium" that stays the same in all episodes. On the other side, a different business is shown to occupy that store front in every episode. Each one has a funny name; examples include the following:

Uncle Marty's Breast Pumps
Hannibal's Dead Animal Taxidermy
A Fridge Too Far—used appliances
Yes, Wire Hangers
Fern, Baby, Fern—discount fern store

3 *The Burger of the Day* Another running gag in most *Bob's Burgers* episodes is the "Burger of the Day" written on the chalkboard behind the counter. These use puns and wordplay and sometimes relate to the plot. The burger is always $5.95. Some examples are as follows:

The Child Molester—comes with Candy
Pepper Don't Preach Burger
Rest in Peas Burger
Foot Feta-ish Burger
Olive and Let Die Burger
She's a Super Leek Burger (comes with braised leeks)

There are, however, a few episodes with no Burger of the Day, mainly when the Belchers don't appear in the restaurant.

One episode directly addresses the phenomena. In *Sexy Dance Healing*, Bob can't come up with any burger puns for his Burger of the Day board. The lack of the Burger of the Day causes a traumatized Teddy to storm out of the restaurant. Even the kids can't handle it. Eventually, while making a regular burger he comes up with the "Running Out Of Thyme Burger" and normal service is resumed.

4 Montages Bob's Burgers uses montages quite a lot to summarize the action and compress time in the episode.

5 End Credits As the end credits play, the show usually finishes with a song that is unique to that episode.

So now we know how *Bob's Burgers* works. Let's look at a specific episode.

The Ring (But Not Scary)

Plotlines

In the episode "The Ring (But Not Scary)," there are two plots:

The A plot: The children have lost an engagement ring (that Bob was going to give Linda for their anniversary) at a water park. Their goal is to find the ring and save their mom and dad's marriage.

The B plot: Linda is trying to apply eye drops to her psychotic sister, who has pink eye from letting her cat sleep on her face.

Act Structure

Bob's Burgers uses the three-act structure but not in the most traditional way. The show tends to have a very long act one. In a twenty-minute show, we would normally expect the end of act one to come in at around five minutes. In this episode, the end of act one is around ten minutes in—nearly half the show length. This is usual for *Bob's Burgers* as they spend time setting up the situation and are not afraid to do quite long verbal jokes in the scenes building up to the act change.

If we follow act one for a moment, in this episode the kids find an expensive engagement ring that Bob plans to give to Linda for their anniversary. It turns out that Bob couldn't afford an engagement ring when they first got engaged and wants to make up for it now—he's even taken out a loan to pay for it. This sets up the value of the ring, both in money terms and in emotional investment. So, when the kids lose the ring at the water park, we know why they are so desperate to find it.

While all this is going on, we also have a physical goal for act one. The ring is stuck on Gene's finger and the kids are trying to get it off. Unfortunately, it falls off when Gene's finger shrivels up in the water and it gets lost at the water park. When we get to the end of act one, the kids state their goal for act two. They vow to find the ring and save mom and dad's marriage "so dad won't end up as a single skank!"

During act two, Bob joins the kids as they search the water park for the ring. This is a fairly simple, physical tickable goal and easy for an audience to follow. Act two finishes when Bob gives up looking for the ring and the direction of the story changes again. Here Bob sets a new goal—to "underwhelm" Linda on their anniversary like he usually does.

This might not seem like the most dynamic goal for the final act, but it does lead us into the touching finale of the show. Linda finds out about the missing ring and tells Bob that they don't need a ring to prove their love.

The B plot is short and simple and follows the three-act structure too. In act one, we learn that Linda's sister has pink eye and needs help putting her eye drops in.

Act two is a great physical comedy routine as Linda does her best to put the drops in her sister's eye, although her crazy sister keeps fighting her off. This act finishes when she gives up trying to put the eye drops in on her own and goes to Bob for help. When she gets home, she discovers Bob and the kids are missing. The new goal for act three, to find Bob and the kids—which she does at the water park.

Set Pieces

There are two montages in this episode. There is a montage condensing the time when the kids visit the water park. In the duration of one song, we feel that we have seen them spend the whole day there. Then, there is a second montage in act two that is used to summarize the search for the ring.

Lastly, as the end credits play and the cast float around in their inner tubes at the water park, the guest character Nat Kinkle (in a tribute to the fact that her name sounds like Nat King Cole) sings a song to the tune of her namesake's hit *Mona Lisa*.[1] The song is dedicated to Linda and called "Mona Linda."

Bob's Burgers: *A Summary*

We can see that anyone hoping to write an episode of *Bob's Burgers* should stick to the three-act structure (although act one would be longer than in other shows), they should use an A and a B plot and use various members of the Belcher family as the leads in both plotlines. They would also need to absorb the off-the-wall style of humor in the show, as well as incorporate the Burger of the Day, montages if necessary, come up with a funny "store next store" for the credits, and find an appropriate title.

All of this might seem like a lot to take in, but the more you immerse yourself into a show, the more it becomes part of the way you think. This is easier in a well-established show like *Bob's Burgers* where there is a huge back catalogue of episodes, but a newer show may take a more detailed analysis when you only have a few episodes to view.

1. Nat King Cole, "Mona Lisa," March 11, 1950, Capitol, 1950, vinyl single.

Chapter 22

COLLABORATION

Writing for animation is perhaps the most collaborative form of writing. When you write a novel, you are the writer and the director, while the reader functions as the performer delivering the lines in their head as they read. When you write for the stage or the screen, you will probably be working with a director and a producer and actors will be interpreting your lines. There will also be set designers, prop makers, and storyboard artists. All of these exist in animation, but it goes one step further. In a live-action show, a character is going to pretty much look like the actor who is cast in the part, whereas in animation the description in your script will give artists the starting point for designing your characters. These are all people who will be reading your script, but who also may be attending meetings and providing feedback (usually called "notes") on your script.

The collaborative process may even go further than that. Several years ago, we were asked to develop a new animation series. When we say new, the concept wasn't new; it had been a cherished and successful series in the past but was going to need a reboot if it was going to get the green light again. We were commissioned to redevelop the idea and write a series proposal (similar to the type seen in Appendix B). Before we started writing, we were asked to come to a meeting to make sure we moved the show in the right direction.

We arrived at the meeting on a Friday afternoon to find ourselves sitting around a huge desk with twelve other people. Two of the twelve were the show's producers, and the other ten consisted of members of the marketing department, the company's book publishing team, the brand team, the DVD distributors (DVDs were still big at this point), the toy team, and someone who deals with apps and online content. Each of these departments was requesting things that needed to be included in the show in order for the series to go ahead. Once the show got the green light, we would be collaborating with the director and the producer, but before we could get that far we would have to satisfy all of these departments.

On other shows we have worked on, we have collaborated with educational advisers, consultants, and broadcasters. As we said in the first chapter, animation is big business and there are lots of people who want to make sure that the show will make its money back. Many writers are uncomfortable with this mingling of art and business, but the more you make friends with the reality of the situation, the easier your life as an animation writer will become.

If you are making a short for the internet and you are planning to animate it yourself and do all the voices, then you won't have to collaborate that much. If you plan to evolve your career further, then at some point you're going to have to collaborate.

Collaboration Means Cooperation and Concessions

When we started writing animation, we had a vision that at some point our genius would be recognized and everyone would just trust our creative vision. That hasn't happened. We are okay with that, because we now realize that was an unrealistic expectation. Whatever your project, there will always be someone who wants to have some input and there is never just one person who is high enough in the pecking order to call all the shots. It's just not the nature of the animation world today.

To get by in animation, you are going to need to find a way to work well with others, and understand where they're coming from and what they need for the project to work for them. It won't always go smoothly, but the better you become at collaborating, the more successful you'll be (and the happier you'll be too).

The problem is, you're going to have to deal with ideas. Did we just say that ideas are a problem? Yes, we did. Let us explain.

Ideas are great. If you're going to be a writer, you're going to need a lot of them. You should never worry about running out of ideas; if you're creative, they just keep coming. Having ideas is like a muscle; the more you generate, the more you have and the easier they come. The problem is, ideas come with a tricky side effect. When an idea goes off in your head, it tends to make you think that it's right. The problem is that it might not be. We've seen writers (and producers and directors) so convinced that their idea is the right idea, even when there is so much evidence to the contrary, that they pursue it and try to keep it in a script to the detriment of the whole production.

Bonus Material: The One-Off Funny Idea

This is a type of idea that we want you to be particularly aware of, and it should be treated with extreme caution. Have you ever been watching a movie and you've thought "it would be hilarious if . . . (insert 'one-off funny idea' here)?" It's quite a fun thing to do. Being a writer you will do this the whole time, hopefully not just with movies but with your own scripts as well. That's good! It might throw out a funny idea that's perfect for the scene you've been writing. The problem can occur when that one idea affects the rest of your story. Suddenly, you find yourself trying to reengineer your whole story to accommodate that hilarious moment into your script. If that makes the story stronger, that's fine, but we've seen writers weaken their stories trying to squeeze in their one brilliant idea because they are convinced it is so funny or clever.

The story should always come first. If the story is strong, the funny moments that are organic to the story structure will always be better than the one-off funny ideas. This is something that you need to be aware of not only with your own ideas but also with ideas that come from other people. There will always be people who have that "one-off funny idea" that they think you should incorporate into your story. If you like it and it makes your story stronger, then good. But beware of restructuring for one funny moment.

The exception to this is in a short sketch, where the one-off funny idea might be the basis of the entire sketch!

So, the idea that you've had that seemed so brilliant might not be as good as you think it is and you may need another. Don't worry, you will have a ton of ideas so don't get precious about that one. But there is another aspect to ideas that you need to be aware of and it's one that can make life difficult. Before we get to that, we want to remind you of two points from earlier in the chapter:

1. There are a lot of people who will have some input into your story.
2. When someone has an idea, they tend to think it's right—even when it might not be.

As a writer, you can be in the difficult situation of several people having conflicting ideas for your script and they all think they're right. You might be working on a student project or maybe making your own show and all your friends are helping you. You could be working for a major production company and everyone thinks your episode should go in a different direction. In all these cases, people are going to be offended if you don't listen to their ideas, and it will make your job an uphill struggle. It doesn't matter what level you are working at—this is a real situation and you will have to deal with it.

There is no one way to deal with these scenarios. Every situation is different, and there will always be a combination of personalities and motivations behind the ideas that you've been presented with, but we've found three principles that help negotiate this minefield.

Listening

When someone is giving you feedback that you know is going to mess up your story, the natural reaction is to start arguing. Sometimes this will be out loud and sometimes it will only be in your head; either way, while that's happening, you're not taking everything they are saying on-board. The person giving you the notes might be right or wrong; the important thing to remember is that they are saying it for a reason. Whatever your views on their feedback, you will do a lot better if you understand their reason for saying what they're saying. This requires listening, asking questions, and engaging in conversation.

Let us give you an example. Some time ago, we were proposing an episode that involved a soap box cart race. There was a major objection from the producer; they didn't want any soap box racing in the series. It seemed like this idea was dead in the water. After some conversation, it turned out that the real objection was to seeing the soap box carts being constructed during the episode—and our idea included a cart building montage. This show was being made in computer-generated imagery, where the cost of constructing complex props was expensive. The budget allowed them to render a couple of completed soap box carts for the race, but the cost of animating the soap boxes at various stages of being built was going to cost too much. The montage was replaced by a scene showing the outside of the workshop, along with some comedic sound effects as the cart was constructed; this was followed by the completed cart being wheeled out and revealed as finished. By engaging in conversation and addressing the real concern, animating the construction process, this episode was green lit.

Diplomacy

When you started reading a book on writing for animation, you probably didn't think you would have to learn about diplomacy. When you are working in TV and Film, a little diplomacy goes a long way. If you want to have any career longevity, you had better be incredibly talented or really nice to work with—or better still both. You could be the most talented writer in Hollywood; if you're not nice to work with, others will be plotting your downfall and will rejoice when it happens.

Without sounding too much like Dale Carnegie, the more friends you have in the business, the better your career will be. Having said that, this is a creative environment and sometimes passions run high; there will be explosions and clashes. When you do finally detonate, do your best to make amends afterward. People rarely hold grudges against people who apologize. Just be nice to work with.

Concessions

Everyone working on a project will have a view on how you should be telling your story; some will be helpful and some won't. Remember though, as the writer you are the person with the overview of how each idea will affect the whole story and the story is your responsibility. When notes come back that you don't agree with, it is important that you pick your battles. Decide which are the story points that are worth fighting for and which points you should concede. If you fight every battle, you will fall under the category of difficult-to-work-with. If you concede every point, the story you end up with will be watered down and lack direction. In the end, if the script isn't good, no one will acknowledge that it was their notes that caused the problem—they're going to blame the writer. You need to protect the story, it is your responsibility and what they hired you for.

Remember, when picking your battles, some departments know more about what will work best in a given situation than the writer does. While you need to be able to think visually to write animation, chances are the director will have a better grasp of the visual aspects of the show than you do. It doesn't mean that they are always right, but it is worth listening to, so you know where they're coming from. Then use diplomacy when you fight your battle to keep them on your side for the rest of your time on the project.

Bonus Material: It's Not Your Fault.

There will be times when you get feedback that decimates your idea. You need to remember, this isn't personal (unless of course you've been seriously undiplomatic in the past, in which case it might be). The other thing you need to remember is that it wasn't your fault (unless of course you did a slack job, in which case it might be).

Notes that send your story back to square one happen all the time in this business. Changes in direction for the show, indecisiveness within the production, and people wanting to change your idea are part of daily life for an animation writer. When you get notes like this, there is no point in beating yourself up about it. There is nothing you could have done. Just be glad that this doesn't happen too often. If it does happen a lot, it is worth considering whether you should look for a new project to work on. It could be that either you are just not getting that particular show, or the production team are a bunch of crazy makers. Both of these things happen, and, again, neither of them are your fault.

Chapter 23

CREATING THE SHORT

The Academy of Motion Picture Arts and Sciences defines the duration of a short animation as a film with a running time of forty minutes or less. This gives quite a scope for short film writing. We have written short films for the internet that are less than a minute long but have also written standalone TV specials that run closer to thirty. While each was quite different, there are processes that can be used to help in writing shorts, whatever length you are working to.

Why Make a Short?

When Paul started out, he wanted to write novels. The books on novel writing at the time all said that you should master the art of short story writing first. In doing so, you learn about the fundamentals of storytelling, character, action, dialogue, and plot without investing the huge amount of time it takes to write a full novel. Short story writing is a quick process compared to a novel that can take years, and, if you're new, chances are that novel won't be good enough to publish. That's because you haven't honed your skills crafting short stories. Well, Paul didn't like short stories so he tried to write novels and, in the end, he wrote two half-finished bad ones. He should have listened to the advice.

Writing short films is like writing short stories. You get to work on your craft without the time investment of writing a full feature film. Telling a good story in ten minutes, five minutes, or even two minutes takes ability and that's an ability that develops with practice.

Initially, you might want to write a short by taking all the principles in this book and applying them to your short film idea. This might work if you were planning to work in the longer end of the short film spectrum, it's even possible to do that in as little as ten minutes, if you're concise and have become adept at conveying information quickly and visually. But you may not want to tell anything as complex as that.

Many short films are the same length as episodic TV shows. We have worked on episodes that fit a five-minute TV time slot, which meant that the body of the episode was only around four minutes long—shorter than a lot of shorts. But you could compare episodic TV writing and short film making in the same way you might compare designing a washing machine with constructing a sculpture out of the parts that make up a washing machine. When you make a washing machine, it normally fits within a set of parameters of size and technical functions. It must work electronically and mechanically and be plumbed in correctly. A sculpture made from the parts can look like an explosion in a workshop or like something that Heath Robinson drew. With the short film, especially an independent one, you are freed from the requirements of broadcast time slot, regular cast, and animation style. You can let your imagination run wild.

How then, do you use what you have learnt in this book to create your short film? Well there is no one set way. To go back to the washing machine analogy again, when you make a sculpture, you have a lot more choice. As such, you need to start with what kind of short animation you are going to make. You may have a duration that you need to adhere to for a particular project, festival, or competition. You may have already decided on the technology that you are going to use. How much of a narrative form is your film going to take, or is it going to be more abstract? Do you already have an idea or are you starting with a blank slate?

Bonus Material: Making an Independent Short

It's now possible to make animations on your smart phone and post them straight to the internet. There are plenty of forums and websites available to showcase your work and even win awards.

If you're reading this because you want to be a director or producer and you want to understand more about story, this is a great chance to make something exactly as you imagine it. If writing is your priority, you may want to team up with others to help you make it. Either way, this is a great way to network, practice your craft, build up your resume, and submit your work to festivals. The likes of George Lucas, Trey Parker and Matt Stone, and, of course, Walt Disney started off making short animated films.

When you make an independent short, it is an opportunity to push boundaries. Use this time to express yourself. Be as subversive or mainstream, funny or dramatic, surreal or conventional as you like—whatever suits your creative leanings.

Finding the Right Tool

While many independent animated short films use edgy artistic visuals, you will find that the ones that employ basic storytelling techniques are often the ones that engage the viewing panels. There are cases of visually stunning animations with very little narrative—see George Lucas's *Look at Life*—but most use some form of story. If you have an idea for your abstract animation that doesn't employ any narrative, then go ahead and make it. Tools and techniques should never outweigh raw talent or the power of an idea. However, if you are going in that direction, we hope the case study at the end of this chapter encourages you to at least entertain the idea of adding some narrative elements to your film. If, however, you are starting with only the beginnings of an idea (or even no idea at all) or you have something that you've fleshed out and you just want to make it a bit better, then we suggest applying some of the principles you have read to expand and/or refine your idea.

We suggest if you are making a showcase film, you start at less than five minutes. Films of this length are quicker to make, so you get feedback on how successful your storytelling has been quite quickly. It is also easier to get people to watch something that is short. As your skills develop, then extend the length of your projects—you will be a better animator and a better storyteller by then. Which tools you use in the writing process will be dependent on your initial idea and the length of the project you are engaging in.

Assuming the idea that you have is going to be narrative rather than abstract—that is after all the scope of this book, to create narrative—we would suggest the use of two particular tools when making a short:

1. Create an emotional connection with the character.
2. Give your character a goal.

Let's look at those two points in the context of short film making.

Create an Emotional Connection with the Character

When you only have a few minutes to tell a story, you don't have long to "grab" the audience. Chapter 10 on Emotional Connection gives you several tools to increase emotional connection with your character; the more efficient you are at getting your viewer to engage with your main character, the more compelling your stories will become.

In Pixar's *Partly Cloudy*, we see clouds making babies for the storks to deliver. It is hard to say whether Peck the stork or Gus the cloud is the lead character, but we have an emotional connection with them both. All the other storks get nice babies to deliver, but Peck gets hazardous ones. As such, he suffers both jeopardy and adversity. Gus on the other hand has little ability when it comes to "making babies." Instead of the cute bundles of joy the other clouds create, he makes a crocodile, a porcupine, and a shark. Here we have a character who is funny because of his ineptitudes, but this also makes Gus sad and we sympathize with him. There is also a caring bond between both characters so we feel that they are both nice and we love them for it.

In the brilliant *Hair Love*, we see something as simple as a young girl who doesn't like her hair. Later we will discover that her mother has cancer, and has lost her hair—which is definitely undeserved misfortune—but the filmmakers have already created a strong emotional connection long before the audience get that information. This is a young girl with crazy hair and she wants it to be pretty. As she tries to tackle the issue of her hair, we see that she has unwavering resolve, she's not going to give up on the hairstyle she loves. She is funny, cute, and on the screen straight away.

In *Bear Story* by Gabriel Osorio Vargas, again we see misfortune as we follow a bear who was taken away from his family to perform in a circus. But even before we learn of that undeserved misfortune, we see that the bear has amazing skills and abilities as he constructs incredible clockwork displays. In *Father and Daughter*, we see a young girl whose father never returns after going out in a rowing boat one day. The whole short film follows her unwavering resolve as she keeps returning to where she last saw her father. Which, in her case, is a lifetime.

Give Your Character a Goal

In a short it is possible to tell a story without a goal being central to the plot, you can watch things "just happening" to a character. Peck in *Partly Cloudy* is one such character, although in the end we see that Peck has the goal of staying with Gus and works toward that by getting some protective clothing so that he can deliver the dangerous "babies" that Gus has created. The aim though is to engage an audience, and a character with a goal is usually more engaging than one without. The shorter your story, the more simplistic and quickly understood by your audience your goal will need to be.

It is easy to forget now, but many of the early *Looney Tunes* and *Walt Disney Productions* were made for theatrical release. These were short films—not part of episodic television—and they focused on simple, physical goals. Whether it was watching Bugs trying to evade the hunter, Sylvester trying to catch the bird, or Goofy trying to surf when the very ocean is against him. The entertainment value of these short films is obvious; many of them still stand up today, and the principle of having a clear and simple goal in animated shorts is still important.

In *Hair Love*, the little girl wants a very specific hairstyle. In *Father and Daughter*, the young girl wants to see her father again. Both are physical, tickable goals. In Jacob Frey's short film, *The Present*, we see a three-legged dog trying to get a child to play with him. This is a very simple setup and goal, but is made original—not to mention very touching—by the reveal at the end, which is that the child has also lost a leg. In *Bear Story*, although the story is told as an embedded narrative, the bear is desperate to get back to his family.

While we would put emotional connection and goals at the forefront when developing your short film, what if you don't have your initial idea yet?

Thinky Time #14

Now we're going to put a few things together. We want you to go back to the character you created in Thinky Time #11. (If you skipped that stage, go back to it now. If you want to create a new character, then just do it again.) Once you have a character ready, focus on two things.

1. The archetype that the character falls under.
2. The ineptitudes that the character has.

Next, remember when you put the character in five interesting situations at the end of that Thinky Time? We want you to do the same thing again, but now make those interesting situations ones that the character wouldn't want to be in, based entirely on their ineptitudes. If your character is a bovine-centric, one step behind bull who is particularly clumsy, they could have a job in a china shop. Our bull is strong and gruff and lacks the elegance he needs to deal with his customers or the delicate products on display. What if they're a pompous droid with high intelligence but has weak, spindly limbs and is sent to load trucks in an anvil factory alongside some powerful loading robots?

You might now find that you haven't given your character enough ineptitudes. If so, just add some more. This is your character to change and adapt as much as you want. Once you have your five situations, choose the one that you connect with the most. Think of one thing that could go wrong in that scenario and work out how your character overcomes it in the end.

Next, look at the tools for creating an emotional connection (chapter 10). Can you apply just one of those to your character when they first appear on the screen? You might find it is there already; often archetype and ineptitude will often bring out those elements naturally.

Turn this into a two- or three-page script using the script guidelines in Chapter 18.

If, when you've finished, you don't think it's funny enough, make "the drop" a bit bigger using the techniques in Chapter 16.

Bonus Material

While this is primarily a comedic device, it is possible to use the same technique to create drama. The more inept a character is, the more they produce comedy. Therefore, it stands that the less inept a character is, the less they produce comedy—and they produce drama instead. Sitcoms are (hopefully) funny, but many of the best ones have touching, heartfelt moments that give us a lump in the throat. Next time you watch a sitcom and it moves you emotionally, notice that the characters in that moment are not being inept.

If you want to use the exercise above to create a dramatic piece, you can simply give your characters abilities in the area in which they are working, not too many; you still want their goals to be a struggle, but by avoiding the "fish out of water" scenario, you create drama instead of comedy.

This exercise might seem simplistic, and in its most basic form it is, but this is an exercise for approaching the blank page, when you just don't know how to proceed. As such, it can give you a good starting point and move you from just being stuck, to having a solid idea in front of you that you can then craft into something great.

Short Film Case Study: "The Meaning of Life" by Don Hertzfeldt

This is a film whose production values are within reach of the independent filmmaker; it also shows what can be achieved when narrative principles are added to an abstract form. There is no obvious central character, very little dialogue—at least not in understandable conversation—and it takes us in unexpected directions. Yet, even a cursory viewing of the film gives us a feeling that we are watching a story of some sort. The stunning art and the rhythm of the film makes this compelling viewing, but let's look at the narrative elements and why they are successful.

Throughout the opening credits, we watch as a person seems to both plummet and fall slowly through the air. We see them as they grow old, die, and decay. Next, as we come out of the opening credits, we see the beginning of life, not a character's life but what would seem to be Earth's earliest life as it crawled out of the ocean in primordial chaos. We see life struggle to evolve, only to then engage in trivial day-to-day life; we see angry exchanges, busy lives spent pointlessly, and then finally death. We have a strong emotional connection to the characters on screen, but why?

This short film uses three of the tools that help create emotional connection to engage the audience in the first couple of minutes of screen time. First, these creatures are funny. This comes from the brilliant artwork, perhaps more than the writing, but we are instantly entertained by the darkly comic anguish of the characters (see Figure 28) as we see both desperation and anger played out. These characters are on the screen right from the beginning, the first one is alone as we watch it mature into a human being. As the creature fights to evolve

Figure 28 *The Meaning of Life*, January 2005.

we see its determination—the alternative, presumably is extinction. So, we see them in adversity too. Once we have this audience empathy, we want to know what happens next.

As multiple characters appear, we might start to question which character we are following. Chances are, this question will only be at the subconscious level, but it is still usually there. But in this case, any individual character is lost in the crowd. This incredible opening sequence makes the audience ask a bigger question, and one that we are set up to ask just by knowing the title of the film, "What is the meaning of life?"

We suggested in the earlier parts of this chapter that the short film is where you can be subversive; you can take things in a creative direction that might be prohibited in an entirely commercial venture. *The Meaning of Life* takes us in such a direction. Instead of the central character appearing on the screen, it is the audience who has the goal for this film—to answer that very question and discover the meaning of life. This question may not be physical, but because we ourselves are the central character, it is most definitely "tickable." If by watching this short film we discover the meaning of life, we will know that we can tick that box. The filmmaker in this case makes you feel that he knows the answer, and if you continue to watch, you might just find out the answer for yourself. From that point on, we are taken on a journey as we pursue that goal. Ultimately we fail. Not all stories have a happy ending.

While *The Meaning of Life* uses many of the principles we have outlined, it has subverted most of them and not least its act structure. If we were to follow the three-act structure in its strictest form, we would follow the same character as they pursued their goals, along with the necessary changes in story direction. *The Meaning of Life* gives us three acts but in a slightly different guise. First, we follow life, we watch a species evolve giving us a simple first-act goal—to survive the evolution process. But then the narrative changes direction, as we lose sight of that single character, we ourselves become the central character as we try to discover the meaning of life. We follow these characters through their life of preoccupation and then to their death. As we spin off the planet and shoot through the galaxy, we are led to believe that maybe we are going to find the meaning of life in the stars. As we travel to distant planets, we discover a myriad of life forms each behaving in the same trivial way as the humans back on Earth, leading us to realize that we are not going to discover the answer to our question. The story now takes us into the third and final act. We watch as a young alien, perhaps with its father, is pondering the same question as we are. As that young creature stares up at the stars, we understand that we are not alone in trying to answer this question. Two changes in direction, or act breaks, three acts.

The Meaning of Life is also a comedy and uses (again subversively) solid comedy structure. We are literally watching the "fish out of water" comedic situation as we follow something evolving from sea life to trying to understand the biggest question of them all. We can also see "the drop" being executed perfectly as the drama takes us through the battle of the evolutionary process, only to hear the first words that we speak "give me your money." Then when we fly through the universe, expecting revelation to occur, we discover aliens behaving the same way that we do. Both of these moments give us a drop in expectation and a drop in status, while the second example also demonstrates a drop in normality.

The Meaning of Life is a stunning film on many levels, and while it is somewhat abstract and definitely subverts the storytelling form, it is worth noting how much more successful the film is precisely because it does use narrative storytelling techniques. We have emotional connection, goals, three acts, and some very solid comedy techniques.

It is hard to know how much of this idea came to Don Hertzfeldt fully formed and which bits he had to craft and rework to get right. If you plan to make mainstream comedy or drama shorts, the necessity of following storytelling fundamentals is obvious, and we strongly suggest mastering these skills to the best of your ability. We hope, though, that this analysis encourages you to look for opportunities to elevate your ideas and to use narrative principles, even in your most subversive and abstract films, to make your stories stronger.

Chapter 24

BREAKING THE FORMAT

So far we have given you a lot of tools that you can use to write an independent short, an episode for an animated show, or even a movie. With the information you have, it would now be possible to take a central character, give them a physical goal for act two, an emotional need and tell a story across three acts and produce something great. But as we have said, this is about tools not rules and it is important to remember that great things can happen when you break the "rules" a little.

To demonstrate, we thought it was worth looking at two very successful animated movies that have unconventional structures, to see how they "broke the rules."

Case Study: Frozen *(Central Character Inconsistency)*

When we went through *Zootopia*, the case study showed a brilliant example of how goals can drive the three-act structure. We saw how in act one Judy Hopps set out to become a cop. She goes through the police academy but only ends up being a meter maid. The physical tickable goal for act two is that she must find Emmitt Otterton in forty-eight hours. She succeeds at this, but it's not a happy ending yet. In act three she must save *Zootopia* by finding out why the predators have gone savage. In *Zootopia*, we have one central character whose physical goals drive the plot from act to act. *Frozen* is different.

Central Character

Due to the success of all the Elsa merchandise, you would be forgiven for thinking that she must be the central character in *Frozen*. You might also think that when you watch the movie. Elsa has the big song in the middle of the film (the one everyone knows!) and has the superpower—

she can wield ice and snow. But she is not the central character, Anna is. Like the relationships in this movie, it's complicated.

Let's have a look at the four-point central character checklist.

Who has the main goal that we follow through the story? The answer is Anna, but it's not entirely straightforward. Anna has the tickable, physical goal for act two, but (as we will see in the section on the act structure) her goals in the other two acts are somewhat lacking.

Who is the most proactive character in the story? Again, this is Anna. Her act two goal is to find her sister. What is unusual about *Frozen* is that, as the central character, Anna is not proactive for most of the final act. Standard story structure would dictate that the central character solves their own problem, and while she might in the end, for most of act three Anna is passive and reactive.

Which character spends the most time on screen? Definitely Anna.

Who changes or learns the most by the end of the story? This is shared between Elsa and Anna. They both learn that love will melt a frozen heart. Everyone was expecting it to be a kiss from one of the male characters that did this, but it turned out to be a selfless act of unconditional love by a sister. Here though, Elsa is the one that really undergoes a change as the action of her sister teaches her how to wield her power as a force for good.

So, we have Anna as a central character but with a few irregularities. Those irregularities continue as we look at the act structure.

Act One

When we look at the functions of act one, we can see how this movie is already breaking away from traditional story structure. The scenes set up our world perfectly; we can see straight away that we're in a fairy tale Scandinavian kingdom and that we will be following the princesses in the castle. It also introduces Anna as the central character, but she is not the one with the biggest problem in the first act. Her parents are dealing with the information that their daughter, Elsa, has dangerous powers. For this reason, Elsa is isolated from her sister. This makes Anna lonely, but her problem isn't as big as her sister's or her parents' problem.

The act one goals are also unusual. While we would normally expect the central character to have a goal that takes us to the start of act two,

Anna has no specific goal. She wants to play with her sister and she wants to build a snowman, but these are both less active than Elsa, who is trying to protect people from her powers. Even Anna's parents have a bigger goal than Anna as they try to protect Anna from Elsa's powers.

When we get to the end of act one, a goal is more firmly established. Elsa flees the castle and Anna sets off to find her sister and bring her back—a specific, tickable, and physical goal for act two.

Act Two

Anna is on a quest to find Elsa and bring her back. As she actively pursues her goal—meeting allies and overcoming obstacles along the way—*Frozen* is back using a more traditional story structure. But then, Anna fails in her goal. This can, and does, happen in many standard three-act stories with a single central character, but as we go into act three, *Frozen* yet again breaks with convention.

Act Three

Anna has been hit in the heart by one of Elsa's ice bolts, and we know from act one that this is very serious. In nearly every successful story, the central character is proactive during the third act, solving his or her own problem. In *Frozen*, the central character is dying and is pretty much a passenger in this part of the story. For most of the third act, Kristoff is trying to save Anna, making him the most proactive character in the third act. But we also see Olaf doing his best to keep her warm and Elsa being held prisoner and trying to escape.

Ultimately, Anna does save the day (with what seems like her dying breath), but in the end both Anna and Elsa learn lessons and evolve as characters.

Frozen is a brilliant story—one of the most successful animations of all time—but despite its mainstream success, *Frozen* uses a subversive structure that plays against the traditional use of central character and goals in the three-act structure.

But does a successful movie need to have a three-act structure?

Case Study: Toy Story 3 *(a Four-Act Structure)*

Another successful movie that breaks form is *Toy Story 3*—not exactly an underground, cult animation. Earlier, we highlighted the importance and domination of the three-act structure in animated movies (and TV series). We encouraged you to master its form and understand it at a deep level. We still think this is very good advice, but to prove that not everything fits neatly into three acts, *Toy Story 3* shows us that a four-act story can be just as successful. Just in case you might be doubting its credentials, it became the highest-grossing animated film of its time and won an Academy Award for best animated feature.

Act One

At the opening of *Toy Story 3*, we see how much Andy loved playing with his toys—especially Woody. We also see a montage of him growing up and now, as the story starts in earnest, Andy is off to college and doesn't want to play with his toys anymore. As his mother pesters Andy to clear up his room, the toys realize that they're never going to be played with again. Andy is going to take Woody to college with him, but the other toys are going to be put in the attic. Unfortunately, there is a mix-up and all the toys (except Woody) nearly end up in the trash. The toys are angry that Andy would throw them away and decide that they want to go to Sunnyside Daycare. They don't believe Woody when he tells them that it was a mistake, Andy wanted them to be stored in the attic and not thrown in the trash. Throughout this act, we see that Woody's emotional goal is to keep everyone together; he doesn't want them to go to Sunnyside, because then Andy will never see them again. So, Woody's physical goal is to get them to stay in the attic, together, so they can be there for Andy.

Woody fails at this goal when they all get locked in the trunk of the car and Andy's mom takes them to Sunnyside. When they get there, Woody is still insisting that they all go back to Andy's house with him, but the others refuse. Sunnyside seems like a nice place and Lotso, the head of the Sunnyside toys, is very welcoming. So, Woody sets off on his own, with the physical goal for act two being established. Woody wants to get back to Andy.

Act Two

Woody tries to escape Sunnyside (hanging on to a kite), but only gets as far as the perimeter. This is where Bonnie, the daughter of Sunnyside's receptionist, finds him and takes him home. Meanwhile, back at Sunnyside, it turns out that things aren't as ideal as they seemed. The toys are horrifically abused by the kids at Daycare, and we discover that Lotso is the villain of the piece.

Back at Bonnie's house, Woody makes friends with her toys. He tells them of his plans to get back to Andy's and they resolve to help him. But before Woody leaves, a chance remark leads Bonnie's toys to tell him all about Sunnyside. Woody hears that it's a place of "ruin and despair" and decides to go back and rescue his friends. This sets up his physical goal for the third (but in this case, not final) act—to rescue his friends from Sunnyside.

Act Three

Woody arrives at Sunnyside and tells the others of his plans to break them out. Act three follows a prison escape/heist format, as the old team get back together again.

Andy's toys are successful in their escape. They have left the confines of Sunnyside, but it hasn't gone as well as they planned. Lotso and his henchmen (or hench-toys) attempt to block their escape. Andy's toys and Lotso all end up in the dumpster, which is then picked up by the garbage truck. This changes the story direction once again, giving us a fourth physical goal and a fourth act. The physical goal for act four is to escape from the trash.

Act Four

The fourth act in *Toy Story 3* gives us the same level of action that we would normally see in the third act of a three-act story. The toys try to avoid being crushed as new trash is tipped into the back of the garbage truck. They end up on a conveyor belt, dodge the shredder, and eventually escape the furnace. They have survived, safe and sound. They just have to get back to Andy. Fortunately, the garbage truck that collects the trash from Andy's street is just leaving.

Coda

Woody's emotional goal from the very beginning has been to keep everyone together. In the end, he abandons his goal of them all staying with Andy and writes him a note, so they all end up at Bonnie's. They have a new kid to play with them and the final shot is of all of Andy's toys together on the porch at Bonnie's house.

Don't Try This at Home

You know those shows that tell you that what you are about to see is performed by trained stuntmen and that it shouldn't be tried at home under any circumstances? Well, we're giving you the same recommendation.

Master the Fundamentals

To be successful in this field, you need to master the craft of writing for animation. The level of mastery that we are talking about is built on getting the basics right. This might not sound as fun as doing the wacky stuff and writing the funny gags that you've thought of, but the better you are at the tools in this book, the more competent your scripts will be.

Let us give you an example. When Paul was younger, he decided to take up tennis. He watched Wimbledon and was captivated when the players played a tricky but spectacular shot. When he started playing, he discovered that he was really good at a backhand drop shot. He loved it when he got the opportunity to play it, and the other player would run toward the net without a chance of getting to the ball in time. What he couldn't understand is why the tennis coach was so set on making sure that everyone could do a competent forehand drive. To Paul, this was the most boring, run-of-the-mill shot in the arsenal of tennis shots. But when it came to playing actual matches, it turns out that the forehand drive is an important fundamental. Paul would watch forehand drives sail past him time and time again, desperately hoping for a chance to play the backhand drop shot—the opportunity for which might come up twice a set.

Think of the tools in this book as a selection of important basics that you can use all the time. It will be no good coming up with a great scene that's really funny but it doesn't fit within a total story structure (unless you're writing a sketch). Master the tools of the trade. Your ability to craft a great physical gag or create fascinating characters will still be there and will shine even brighter when you place them into your solid script.

Big Movies, Big Teams

Movies like *Frozen* and *Toy Story 3* do break away from a lot of the real basics in storytelling, and a lot of writers will tell you why they think

Frozen doesn't work. Try telling that to the zillions of kids who think it's the greatest movie ever. Now, take some time and watch the credits at the end of any major animation movie. What we want you to do is look at the writing staff involved. In most cases, there will be several people credited with the script, but there is often also a Head of Story or a Script Editor. Look for anything that implies writing or stories and you will see that a whole host of people have been involved in getting the script from concept to screen. In most cases, these will be people with a strong background in storytelling who have mastered the basics. Between them, they will have told enough stories to have a deep story instinct and know when you can bend the rules and when you need to rely on the fundamentals.

Chapter 25

HOW TO LAUNCH YOUR CAREER

If you talk to writers of animation, you will find that each of them has a different story about how they cracked their way into the industry. For some, it would have come through social networking and others an accidental meeting; some might have been working in another area of animation (a good friend of ours was a production manager first), and others might have been pitching new show ideas at a conference. There is no one way to get your big break. If you're trying to launch your career, we recommend that you try all of the above and anything else you can think of. So, what's our top tip?

Write the best sample script you can. Preferably more than one. We are asked time and time again how you land your first writing job, as if there is a magic formula. The magic formula is having good sample scripts that you can send out. In that respect, the previous parts of this book are much more important than this chapter. They can guide you toward writing the knockout script you need. For a producer to take a risk on you, you have to be able to prove you can write and your sample script is how you do that.

It's important to clarify here what "risk" the producer is taking when he commissions a new writer. Understanding how the industry works will give you a much clearer idea of why it is so hard to land that first job. The path you take if you want to write a movie is a little different to the one you take if you want to write episodic television, but if you're going to make a living as a writer of animation, chances are you are going to work in both. You might need to write several episodes of a TV show before anyone will read your movie scripts. Also, the development stage of a movie can be long and slow, and writing episodes for a TV show is a good way to keep writing, learning, and supplementing your income during that process.

Bonus Material

While you are working in episodic television, you will also be networking and meeting people in the industry. Everyone you meet will talk to others who work in animation; and the more people who like you, the more work you will get. Remember, this includes those who are only just starting their career, the interns and office juniors of today will be the producers and directors of tomorrow.

Writing Episodic Television

When a show goes into production, there is an incredibly tight schedule that the show runs to. As a writer, your first job is normally to pitch ideas for an episode that you would like to write. If they like one of your ideas, you'll be asked to expand this to a one-page premise, where you summarize how the plot will develop in your proposed episode. Once the "powers that be" (usually the producers and the head writers) are happy with that premise and want to see it as an episode, you get commissioned. Congratulations, you have a job and a contract is issued.

The next stage is usually to write an outline for your episode. This is longer than the premise and will include the individual scene headings. The outline is usually around four to six pages for a ten-minute show. You will then keep revising the outline until everyone is happy that the story is working. Once everyone is happy with the story, you then move on to first draft script. Once you are at script stage, there is a second-draft script that deals with any structural problems that have arisen and a script polish that normally involves making final adjustments to dialogue. At each stage of scripting, you will receive feedback and notes from the various "powers that be." Each show is different, but these "powers" can include head writers, producers, the director, broadcasters, and educational advisors.

At last, the final draft of the script is delivered. This process will normally take around five or six weeks.

Six weeks might sound like a long time to write a ten-minute episode of a cartoon, but it can be a frantic time. You won't be writing for that full six weeks as you will often be waiting for feedback and sometimes the feedback is delayed. Often, the feedback will seem inconvenient as your episode will need a restructure. This may take longer than you expected and sometimes will appear late in the process.

While unexpected changes can be annoying, remember the head writers, and the producers will be juggling up to eight scripts at the same time from the whole team of writers. They will be trying to make all of the stories work together, they will want a good variety of themes, locations, and characters across the series. They might also be dealing with budgetary issues and marketing requirements (remember all those departments we told you about?). There is also a delivery schedule, where the team need to complete scripts on time. This schedule will vary from show to show, but in recent series the normal delivery rate has been one completed script a week.

Once your episode has been delivered, it will go out to the storyboard artists who will start the visual process, and it will also be recorded by the voice artists. The voice artists are booked when an episode is commissioned, so any delay with your script can cost the production company cancellation fees for both actors and the recording studio.

While the process on each show will vary slightly, you can now see difficulties in the process and the importance of delivering a script on schedule. This is why producers are often reluctant to give new writers a try. You are untested and they have no idea how you will cope with last-minute restructures or how fast you can deliver a script if the notes are delayed. Head writers will be the ones who have to spend the weekend rewriting a script that didn't work in the end, so they tend to only work with writers they trust.

All of this means that the way you land your first job is to go from being an untested writer to a writer who is considered to be a safe pair of hands. And for that, once again, you need good sample scripts. The more outstanding your scripts are, the better it is. Some shows will ask you to write an "audition" script as well, to see if you "get" that particular show. Don't be offended if you're asked to do this. The fact that a production company has taken the time to offer you a chance and is going to read your script is a massive opportunity.

Writing a Movie

First a reality check. To date, we have never heard of a writer bringing an unsolicited script for an animated movie to a production company, and the movie has made it to the screen in the way that writer imagined at the beginning. This might have happened somewhere, but we've never heard of it.

An animated movie might start off in any number of ways. It could be a visual concept, a character design, a book, an existing TV show, a game, or just someone's vague idea. The way you normally end up writing a movie is that someone comes to you with their idea and they commission you to write it. More often than not, this wasn't your idea in the first place. As we've said before, animation is a collaborative medium.

If you want to be commissioned to write a movie script, you need to prove that you can do it. If you can prove that you can structure a good story, make people laugh, and make people feel for your characters across a script that is 80–100 pages long, you have a better chance of landing the job. Like working in television, you're going to need a sample script.

The writing process is pretty much the same as an episode from a TV show. You will most likely write a premise, several drafts of an outline, and probably several drafts of the script. One of the key differences is that you may not have a deadline. Quite often the rest of the production process will not be booked until everyone has signed off on the script. This means that it can be a lengthy process and patience is essential— the reason why a lot of movie writers also write episodic television.

Writers' Groups

A writers' group is a group of like-minded people who all want to be better writers and joining such a group is a great way to make sure your sample scripts are up to scratch. As part of the group, you write scripts (or outlines for scripts), send them to each other, read the scripts, and give each other feedback. These can be people that you meet up with on a personal level, but they can also be an online group that uses a forum or even video conferencing.

The one thing you need when you are starting out is honest feedback. It's great getting your family and friends to read your work, but there are three reasons why you should not go to them for feedback:

1. Family and friends rarely give you the brutally honest feedback that you need. But, you will find that members of a writers' group want to prove they understand story principles, so will only be too happy to point out where they think you've gone wrong.
2. If your family or friends give you brutal feedback, there is a high chance you will take it personally. You might end up having some

heated exchanges in your writers' group, but it doesn't really matter.
3. Unless your family members are aspiring writers, or work in the TV and film industry, they probably don't know which bits of feedback are most useful.

This might make a writers' group sound like a hostile environment, and in one respect it is. They will tell you what they don't like about your script. But that is exactly what you need. When you're writing for a living, directors, producers, and other writers will be highlighting these problem areas for you. Until you get there, you need someone else to give you that feedback. It also toughens you up for the feedback you'll get when you're working!

Once you are in a writers' group, there a few things you can do to make your time as effective as possible.

1. When you give feedback, be prepared for the fact that the other person might disagree with your notes. This can be frustrating if you can see where someone is going wrong, but the best you can do is try to help them and then let it go. Some people just don't want to make the changes; they just want to hear how good their script is (don't be that person).
2. When you get feedback, make a note of all of it but don't assume that all of it is right. Everyone will have a vision of what they think you should do with your script, but it's you that has to decide on what story you want to tell.
3. The group is there to help you discern if your story is working or not. If your story isn't working, it should help you find the weaknesses but it's up to you to fix it yourself. You might use some of the suggestions that you hear, but don't feel like you have to use it all. As the writer, you need to bring the whole story together and make it work.

Networking

Once you're in a writers' group and you've got some great sample scripts, the next thing you need to do is get people to read your scripts. This requires networking. Talk to as many people as possible and use social media as much as you can. Make friends in the industry. Even when you have a friend that is keen to read your script, it might take longer than you expect for them to get around to it. Sometimes months. Now, you should see the importance of having a really great script. It's going to take a lot of effort to get someone to read your work; the last reaction you want your script to illicit is, "This is terrible! I never want to read this person's stuff again!" If this happens, you need to start both the writing and the networking all over again.

When someone in the industry reads your work and likes it, the most likely response is, "Have you got anything else I can read?" They want to make sure that your script isn't just a one-off. This is why you need to keep writing and have as many great scripts in your drawer (or on your hard drive) as you can.

What to do While You're Trying to Get Your Big Break

As you can see, getting your break might take a while. Fortunately, there are more opportunities than ever before to work in animation. There are children's channels, TV movies, streaming services, theatrical releases, and now online content. This means there are lots of script opportunities as well as other jobs inside the industry. It might take a while to get people to read your stories, but if they know you as someone they've already worked with, they're more likely to listen to you. If you can't get a job straight away, become an intern or a runner. One writer we know started off as a runner and then landed a job in the script department. Initially, he was just photocopying and compiling scripts, but then moved into script editing and soon landed his first job as a writer.

Lastly, you may be wondering about getting an agent. You should pursue this as well as the other areas that we have suggested, as an agent can accelerate your career. But don't get disheartened if you can't get one to start with. Agents make their money from writers and directors (or performers) who are working. They know how hard it is for a writer to get that first job. The cold hard fact is, they don't want to do that work unless they're certain you're going to earn a lot of money. Ideally, they want to sign you just after you become successful so they don't have to lay all the ground work. This might seem unfair, but look at it from their point of view. Would you want to do all that work of landing someone their first job only to find out that they're not going to stick with it? Cultivate relationships with agents alongside all your other networking. It is time well spent, and the good ones will give you advice along the way, even if they're not ready to sign you yet.

Chapter 26

FINAL WORD

After more than twenty years of writing professionally, we still get excited about creating something new. The moment, at the end of the day, when we realize that something exists that didn't when we started that morning is simply magical.

It would be easy to forget that twenty years ago, that blank page was something we considered to be intimidating. The pressure to not only fill it with something but something that would be considered good enough to put on a screen could be overwhelming. There are times when ideas just write themselves, words just spill out of the characters' mouths, and every scene dissolves seamlessly into the next. Then there are other times when coming up with the simplest idea can feel like you are pulling teeth. That's when the principles and tools that we have outlined in this book really come into their own, because now, when you're stuck, all you need to do is work out which is the right tool to use.

This comes with a word of warning though, that is, finding the right tool isn't always easy. We have often spent long hours using the wrong tool for the job. We recently spent most of a day trying to apply act two principles to a story that wasn't working only to discover that the problem was that we didn't have a central character. The tools in this book can help you a lot, but unfortunately there isn't a shortcut. If it was easy, many of the blockbuster animations that we see at the movie theaters wouldn't take five years to make. The good news is that the more you do this, the easier it gets.

The world of animation is an exciting place to be, with advances in technology constantly pushing the boundaries of what is possible. It is also a medium where storytelling techniques continue to evolve and both comedy and drama explore new frontiers. Animation caters for a wide audience, from the simplest preschool concepts, to high-budget animations and subversive artistic productions. In such a big world, it is important to remember that no one writer is the complete package. As your career progresses, you will find that your writing voice starts to emerge and you will discover your strengths. We encourage you to develop those strengths and abilities and work out how to best use them, so that you can find your place in—and contribute to—this exciting world. The only way to do that is to write.

So, start writing and keep writing and then write some more. The world of animation needs you.

APPENDIX A

SCRIPT FORMAT

When you start writing scripts, you'll need to familiarize yourself with the script format and terminology that is used in scriptwriting. Scriptwriting software will move you effortlessly through the format as you write, but it's always a good idea to know what it is you want your audience to see. The more familiar you are with the terminology, the more dynamic and professional your script will look. You can see examples of script format in Figures 19 and 23, and we have covered the basics in Chapter 18, but this appendix gives you a comprehensive guide to all of the script elements that are available to you.

Scene Headings

You will always begin each scene with a scene heading. Scene headings are in capital letters and perform the following functions:

a) Tells the reader whether the scene is inside or outside
b) Tells the reader where the scene is taking place
c) Tells the reader what time of day it is

Let's start with inside or outside:

> EXT. represents a scene that is taking place outside.
> INT. represents a scene that is taking place inside.

> You then follow that with the location of the scene, so the scene heading could expand to:

INT. JIMMY'S HOUSE

You would then follow that with the time of day your scene takes place:

INT. JIMMY'S HOUSE - DAY

The reader would know that this scene is going to take place inside Jimmy's house during the day. Or, if you wanted to be more specific, you can include an area within the location by adding a slash:

```
INT. JIMMY'S HOUSE/BATHROOM - DAY
```

Action

You would then follow your scene heading with what is called the action or stage direction. The action tells the reader what they are seeing within the scene. The action is always aligned to the left margin and uses standard upper- and lowercase letters. A scene heading followed by some action might look like this (note the line space between the heading and the action):

```
INT. JIMMY'S HOUSE/BATHROOM - DAY
Jimmy looks in the mirror as he brushes his
teeth, Jenny appears behind him.
```

Character

The next thing we need is dialogue. But before we get to the character's words, we need to know who is doing the talking. At first glance, the character names might look like they are centered but they are indented and left aligned. There is no need to know the exact position as your script writing application will do this for you automatically.

We know the location, the time, and what we can see in the scene. If we want to continue from the previous example, the script now looks like this:

```
INT. JIMMY'S HOUSE/BATHROOM - DAY
Jimmy looks in the mirror as he brushes his
teeth, Jenny appears behind him.


                    JENNY
```

We now know that it's Jenny who is about to speak.

Dialogue

The dialogue has its own set of margins, indented from the action, and is in upper- and lowercase. It looks like this:

```
               JENNY
     Any chance I could use the sink?
```

Usually this is enough, a name followed by a line or a few lines of dialogue, but sometimes, before the actual dialogue, you may want to use some of these abbreviations:

```
(V.O.)
```

The abbreviation for Voice-Over (V.O.) is used when the person speaking the dialogue can be heard by the audience, but not by anyone in the scene. For example:

```
              JENNY (V.O.)
     I never understood why Jimmy would
     always take so long brushing his teeth.
```

```
O.S. (O.O.S. or O.C.)
```

This is the abbreviation for Off Screen (or sometimes Out Of Shot or Off Camera). O.S. is used when the character is speaking off screen but the other characters within the scene can hear them. For example: if they are outside a door:

```
              JENNY (O.S.)
     Okay Jimmy, I'll wait outside till
     you've finished brushing your
     teeth.
```

Parenthetical

Parenthetical refers to a word, or words, in brackets that are inserted between the character name and the line of dialogue (or sometimes between two lines of dialogue). These indicate how a character should deliver their lines. For example:

```
               JIMMY
              (angry)
     Why did you eat my cookies!?
               (sad)
     I loved those cookies . . .
```

You can use emotions such as (happy) (excited) or (exasperated), although we recommend that you only use these if absolutely necessary.

Voice actors are pretty good at getting the emotions right and something as simple as (sadly) won't really sum up the subtlety that they will be aiming for.

You can also use things that might be going on physically, like (out of breath), (chewing/talking with mouthful), or (through loud hailer). The key point is to make sure that the words in parentheses only relate to how the line is delivered—this is not the place to sneak in a stage direction.

Now for a couple of dialogue devices that may come in handy.

The Beat

Usually written as (BEAT). Use this if you want a pause or an interruption in the dialogue. Often used for comic effect when it takes a moment for a character to realize what another character is saying or what is actually going on:

```
                    JENNY
       Kate has the most stupid ugly nose
       I have ever seen. . .
                    (BEAT)
       She's standing behind me isn't she?
```

The Incomplete Sentence

There are two types of incomplete sentence and each one is indicated in a different way.

Sometimes a character just trails off in the middle of a sentence. This can be because they have seen something that shocks or distracts them, or possibly they are just the sort of people who lose focus. This type of incomplete sentence is finished with an ellipsis (three dots . . .).

```
                    JENNY
       I was just thinking, about the
       Ummm . . . you know, the errrr. . .
```

The other type of incomplete sentence comes when someone gets interrupted as they are speaking. This could be because of another character speaking, a loud sound or an action that's taking place within the scene. In this case, we put the unsaid words in brackets. This way the performer knows what the full sentence would have been, had they been able to finish speaking:

```
                    JENNY
        Oh I do love a brisk walk
        especially when it's a [lovely
        day]

Jenny falls down an open manhole.
```

Directing on the Page

That is the basics and, most of the time, that will be all that you need. The scene heading, the action, and the dialogue cover the essentials required to write your script. There will be times however, that you feel like you need to "direct on the page." This should only be done if you need to clarify how a scene could be played out and only if it is relevant to the story. It is not our place as writers to direct, although sometimes it might be necessary to include a close-up to give emphasis to a piece of information, or a point-of-view shot so we know what a character is seeing. The following devices are all available to you, but should be used sparingly (unless you are the director). A script that lists every shot (or one that directs every line of dialogue) will mark you out as an amateur.

Shots

A shot is a single continuous angle, or view, that only shows a specific part of what is happening in a scene. There are a wide variety of shots available to a director, but as a writer there are a few basic shots that can be used to inform the reader what it is you want them to see in the frame.

CLOSE-UP:
This is usually abbreviated to CU. This is a shot where an object or, more usually, a person's face fills the screen. The script might read as the following:

```
CU: Jenny looks shocked.
```

Figure 29 shows a close-up of The Judge in *ParaNorman*, but you can go closer with an Extreme Close-Up (ECU). Figure 30 shows an Extreme Close-Up of Norman from the same film.

```
ANGLE or ON:
```

This directs the camera to be pointed (or angled toward) a particular character or object. It can be used to give emphasis without going for the full close-up. An example would be:

```
ON Jimmy as he turns around to face Jenny.
```

Figure 29 *ParaNorman*, August 5, 2012.

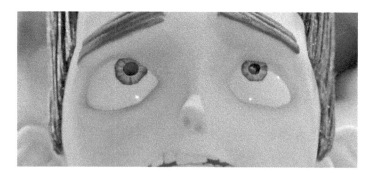

Figure 30 *ParaNorman*, August 5, 2012.

Figure 31 *Despicable Me*, June 27, 2010.

Figure 31 shows an example of how the "Angle" or "On" would work in a scene. This shows a scene from *Despicable Me*. Here, the camera is focused on the cookie bowl while a conversation continues in the background. This action could be missed if the camera wasn't pointed directly at it, especially as the characters in the scene are looking in the other direction.

POV:

We see what the character sees from their point of view, for example:

JENNY'S POV: Jimmy staring back at her as he cleans his teeth.

ESTABLISHING SHOT:

A shot that tells us where the following scene is going to take place. An establishing shot of the New York skyline, for example, would indicate that the next scene or sequence will take place in New York. It can be more specific than that, an establishing shot of a large building with a sign overhead that says, "Bank," would indicate that we are about to go into a scene set in a bank. An example would be:

EXT. THE WHITE HOUSE - DAY

ESTABLISHING SHOT of the White House.

INT. THE WHITE HOUSE/OVAL OFFICE - DAY

The President sits at the desk.

Figure 32 *Cars*, May 26, 2006.

Figure 32 shows an example of an establishing shot from *Cars*. We see this shot outside of the courthouse, which establishes where the following action will be taking place.

Transitions

After you have finished your scene, you will then need to **transition** to another scene. And, of course, there are several ways of doing that. These are in capital letters and are aligned to the right margin.

                                                        CUT TO:

This is the most commonly used transition and is a change of scene over one frame. You can usually omit the CUT TO (although some productions include them for timing purposes). If there isn't any other kind of transition at the end of the scene, CUT TO is always implied.

                                                  SMASH CUT TO:

Like the CUT TO but faster, quite often used for comedic effect.

                                                   DISSOLVE TO:

As one scene fades out, the next scene fades in. This is most commonly used if there is a passage of time between scenes.

                                                  MATCH CUT TO:

When the following shot is almost the same as the shot before. For example: Your first shot is a painting of a seaside scene on a poster.

Then you MATCH CUT to the next shot, and it's the ACTUAL seaside that the painting represents. Add a couple of <SEAGULL CALLS> and you have a perfect MATCH CUT.

Effects

To denote a sound or visual effect, use pointy brackets on either side of the suggested sound or visual effect, usually inserted within the action. For example:

```
Jimmy lights the fuse, it <FIZZLES> for a few
seconds. Then <KABOOM!> the firework <EXPLODES>
in front of him.
```

The Montage

This is a useful device to denote progress or time passing. If you have an eleven-minute script and someone needs to learn to play the ukulele or become a master at Kung Fu, you cannot show this in real time. So, you would use a MONTAGE. A series of short fast-cut scenes with appropriate music. A great example is the Montage Song in *South Park*[1] (see Season 6 Episode 2: *Aspen*).

A MONTAGE can also be used as a FLASHBACK. The opening sequence in the film *Up* has been referred to as a cultural milestone. It shows Ellie and Carl's relationship till her sad demise and it's a masterclass in the power of judicious editing alongside beautifully written music.

1. DVDA, "Montage," *South Park*, Season 6 Episode 2: *Aspen*, Comedy Central, First Broadcast March 13, 2002, TV Program.

APPENDIX B

SAMPLE SCRIPT BIBLE

Understanding a script bible is a fundamental part of writing for animated TV shows. If you are working on a show, these will be provided to you by the production company. If you are creating your own show, you will need to write one of your own so that everyone understands your show and can visualize how it will play out. There is no set format for a script bible, but they usually include the following:

1. An introduction to the show concept. This will tell people everything they need to know about the basic concept and flavor of the show.
2. Descriptions of the main characters.
3. Descriptions of the main locations within the show.
4. Sample storylines.

Script bibles normally evolve as the show progresses, so if you are starting work on a brand-new series, chances are it will be pretty short. If there are already 100 episodes out there, it might be quite extensive as new characters, locations, and story summaries are added.

This appendix shows a sample script bible for your reference. It is for a show that we pitched several years ago that never came to fruition. It is however, a good example of the kind of script bible you can expect to work from—or the type you need to produce if you're creating your own show.

"THE EARTHLINGS HAVE LANDED!"

An Intergalactic Animated Comedy for Six- to Eight-Year-Olds

by Laura Beaumont and Paul Larson

Moving to a new home is never easy . . . making new friends is always hard . . . but coming to terms with a completely alien culture, can be a total nightmare. . .

"THE EARTHLINGS HAVE LANDED!"

follows the fortunes of a modern Earth family as they discover a whole new life . . . on a whole new world.

10 . . . so who is this family?
They're the Twiggs from Illinois. There's Molly (14), Matt (12), Gem (mom) (best not mention her age), and Axl (dad) (as old as he feels).

9 . . . and where is it they've landed?
The town of Neptune on the planet Poseidia (head toward the edge of the known universe and turn left at Pluto). Poseidia is a peace-loving society, where all creatures are equal, everyone lives in harmony, and everything is shared. There is no TV, no movies, no smartphones, and the fastest food you'll find is a hastily passed plate of kelp cookies. Poseidia is untainted by consumerism, media hype, video games, or fashion. Similarity is celebrated and competition is nonexistent.

How dull is that for a pair of Earth kids? The Poseidians live by a simple three-part code (again with the dull!):

1. Shoal first, self last.
2. When the tide rises let it come. When it goes out, . . . let it go.
3. Kelp all year, keeps your blowhole clear.

8 . . . did you say blowhole?
Yes, you see the Poseidians are not THAT different to humans. They walk on two legs and live on the land. But they just happen to be blue, have domed foreheads, and the previously mentioned blowhole. Well,

that's how you tend to look when you evolve from dolphins instead of apes. The Poseidians are enthusiastic, uncynical, and accepting of everything—everything that is, except *change*. And a whole shoal of change has just arrived in the shape of a family called Twigg.

7 . . . so how did the Twiggs get there?
Good question. Basically . . . they won the latest all new/cutting edge/reality/fly on the wall/interactive/gameshow: *"Blastaway!"* Where viewers vote for the family they'd most like to see surviving (or not) in outer space (sponsored by the World Space Program and Snikky-Snax). The idea was that they would be orbiting the Earth in the Blastmaster 1, a space shuttle with hidden cameras on board filming them trying to live their normal, day-to-day lives, in space. Unfortunately, a freak accident sent the shuttle veering off course and through a wormhole where it crash-landed on the planet Poseidia.

6 . . . so what is Poseidia like?
Fortunately, the inhabitants of Poseidia breathe oxygen, but other than that it's a different world out there.

5 . . . but surely "Blastaway" put an expert on board?
You'd think. Actually . . . the Twiggs did have the opportunity to win their own robot—courtesy of *"Blastaway's"* Build-a-Bot round. But, due to their lame score, they ended up with a puke-colored swing-bin on wheels called Cosgrove Glitch the Third.

4 . . . so will the kids make new intergalactic friends?
Of course! There's Dorsal (female)—(908 podyears), Crustacia (female)—(899 podyears), and Welk (male)—(700 podyears).

3 . . . and what about the adults?
There are Welk's parents Mr. Mussel (4,450 podyears) and Mrs. Mussel (4,200 podyears), and Ms. Gourami (3,000 podyears), the Shoal School's only teacher. There's also Miss Finn (2,602 podyears), who runs the General Store, and the Octopus Counselor Guy (OCG)—(12,000 podyears), who we only ever see in tentacle-filled glimpses.

2 . . . so how will the Twiggs fare?
Well . . . they will learn a lot about themselves, their values, and how to adapt to a different culture. Molly will throw herself into Poseidian society with gusto. Matt will embark on the mothership of scam-fests.

Gem will try and find an alternative career to designing Apps. Cosgrove will learn to stop saying, "I didn't ask to be created!" And Axl will find that one planet's incompetent handyman is another planet's mysterious and interesting visitor.

1 . . . and what about the Poseidians?
They'll learn craterloads! Like how to have fun, that competition can be inspiring, and that someone without a bluey tinge can be attractive. They'll also learn that swimming with humans isn't all it's cracked up to be; they'll learn how to "flip the fin" and tell teachers to "stick it down their blowhole." They'll also learn that looking different isn't that scary, that rock'n'roll is good for the sole and, most importantly, . . .that change isn't so bad after all.

Lift off!!!
So it's Twiggs in space—as Britain's first intergalactic family embark on their own personal Poseidian Adventure

"THE EARTHLINGS HAVE LANDED!"

The Twiggs are an unremarkable family from an unremarkable town on an unremarkable planet, which is exactly why they got chosen to be contestants on everyone's favorite new/cutting edge/reality/fly on the wall/interactive/gameshow: "**Blastaway!**"

Characters

Earthlings

Molly (14)   Molly is an optimistic fourteen-year-old whose main aim in life is to keep her crazy family from getting even more crazy. Molly is good-hearted and supportive and always tries to see the best in everyone. She's bright and clever and a hard worker, ever hopeful that one day her dad will fix the Blastmaster 1 so the Twiggs can return to Earth. Having said that, Molly is the one person that truly tries to embrace the Poseidian lifestyle, but it's an uphill struggle getting anyone else in her family to join in. Molly is very fond of her newfound Poseidian buddies but she still misses all her friends back home. So, until she finds herself back there once again, she will continue writing her log and doing everything in her power to embrace her new life.

Matt (12) Matt is a twelve-year-old serial prankster and the bane of Molly's life. A chaotic cocktail: two parts Bart Simpson, one part Tom Sawyer with a twist of Cartman thrown in. Matt is impulsive and determined. If he has a new idea or a plan or a scheme, there is nothing anyone can do to stand in his way. And he's not always alone. Matt's persuasive energy draws people to him like moths to a flame, so there are always people willing to go along for the ride . . . until they realize they are heading down the side of a black-run crater or they've just handed him their allowance! If Matt could use his power for good instead of chaos, he could be the president of the United States, but unfortunately Matt will always be drawn toward the dark side . . . as it's always going to be way more fun!

Gem (Mom) (Best not mention the age) Back on Earth, Gem was an App designer. Her most famous App was Strawberry Squash, which, due to the phenomenal success of Candy Crush, ended up in the App equivalent of the bargain pail, something she has never quite got over. On Earth, Gem would always pride herself in her ability to juggle home life and work but there is no call for Apps in Poseidia, so she is constantly trying to channel her creativity into designing new things that she hopes the people of Poseidia will like. Gem is a perfectionist and can get very anxious if things are out of place, so her chaotic family will always be her ultimate challenge.

Axl (As old as he feels) Axl is the least handy handyman that anyone could ever imagine, but he has big dreams. He believes that one day he will fix the Blastmaster 1. Even though most of his efforts so far have resulted in either an explosion or something falling off the ship's exterior. His methods might be a bit off the wall (like most of the pictures he's tried to hang up), but Axl is ever optimistic and always happy to lend people a hand. He is charming and childlike and loves his family. Just don't ask him to put up any shelves.

Cosgrove Glitch the Third: A Robot Cosgrove is the family's robot. He was designed in the Build-a-Bot round on Blastaway. He speaks like a character from Downton Abbey, is pretentious and arrogant, and clearly feels superior to everyone and everything. He has only been programmed with the contents of "Mrs Battenberg's Book of Home Baking and Household Management" so is incredibly good at cooking and a great help with the household chores—although, it goes without saying, an engineering droid would have been much more useful. He can't repair the space shuttle but he can get a mean shine on the particle accelerator.

Poseidians Poseidians basically look like humans with a dolphin-centric twist. Domed foreheads, small blowholes, and a bluey tinge is pretty much all that separates young Poseidians from Humans. As they get older, their features become more extreme as can be seen by the large moving tentacle that grows out of Miss Finn's head. The language is different but courtesy of Esperanto Ear Drops, (administered to the humans when they arrived) the Twiggs can now understand every word that's said . . . and so can we!

Dorsal (Female)—(908 Podyears) Dorsal is a young Poseidian UFO spotter. She's been prophesying the Earthlings will land for a very long time, she's written essays on the subject, done speculative drawings, walked around with a placard and now she's hit pay-dirt! She is so happy to not only finally meet Earthlings but also be their friend. Her fellow Pod mates have been putting up with her UFO mania for so long; they were pretty much convinced that she was as mad as a bag of Squiddles (small hyperactive Poseidia creatures that don't like being in bags). But with the arrival of the Earthlings, things are beginning to change.

Crustacia (Female)—(899 Podyears) Crustacia is very direct, blunt, and outspoken. Unusual character traits considering she's both Poseidian and the healer in the shoal. Crustacia is constantly exploring alternative healing methods from coral back rubs to kelp flotation tanks and is always on the lookout for folk to help her test them, which can be quite a traumatic experience. Crustacia has no time for malingerers and believes in tough love. She is quick-witted, condescending, and sarcastic.

Welk (Male)—(700 Podyears) Welk is always desperate to impress. Despite his young age, his role in the shoal is "ambassador" to the grown-ups. In other words, he has to keep the communications open between parent and child, a very important role in Poseidian society. Welk is proud of his role and takes it very seriously indeed. Unfortunately, most of his peers aren't very happy about their antics being reported to their mums and dads, and it's not long before Matt is pointing out that on Earth an "ambassador" to the grown-ups would be called something like a "tattle tale." Welk has a sneaky admiration for the Earth children and always tries to be part of the gang . . .

Mr. Mussel (Male): Mayor of Poseidia   Mr. Mussel is Welk's father and a walking talking textbook of all things Poseidian. His job is to look after the Twigg family, help them fit into their new shoal as painlessly as possible, and acclimatize them with the locals down at the Kelp-U-Like. Unfortunately, his ambitions outweigh his natural ability, and although he tries to protect the culture of his planet vehemently, his attempts to try and do everything by the book can sometimes lead to total confusion.

Mrs. Gourami (Female): The Shoal School Teacher   Mrs. Gourami is Matt's nemesis and the only person on Poseidia that he's scared of. She is stern and strict and seems to be able to read his mind. But she does have a dry sense of humor and can sometimes surprise her pupils with energetic displays of extreme Poseidian sports.

Miss Finn: Owner of "Kelp! Kelp! Kelp!"   Miss Finn runs the Neptune General Store (aka "Kelp! Kelp! Kelp!"). Although at first glance she appears to be one of the more extreme characters in Poseidia (mainly due to the moving tentacle on the top of her head), once you get to know her, you realize that she is one of the most practical, smart, and knowledgeable characters there. She is very proud of her store and loves nothing more than trying to get hold of the "un-sourceable." When not there, she'll be out on the surface of Poseidia looking for new things to sell or use as ingredients. At night, she will sit on her roof, Kelpfizz in hand, looking up at the stars through a telescope.

Octopus Counselor Guy (OCG)—(2,000 Podyears)   We never see him properly, but can perceive roughly what he looks like through glimpses of writhing tentacles. But, by means of a video-com, he will help the Twiggs work through any traumas they may have, record their activities, and register their complaints (these usually revolve around Poseidia's main source of nutrition—the ubiquitous kelp).

The Firds   The Firds are a flock/shoal of crazy creatures. They are like a cross between a bird and a fish, and they fly around creating general havoc. Occasionally, they will murmurate into extraordinary shapes in the sky, . . . but most of the time they just create havoc. Having fun is their one aim, and, in the world of Poseidia, they have achieved almost sacred status. Which means they can do whatever they want and no one is allowed to stop them. The Poseidians just try to keep a cheery exterior, no matter how irritating the Firds become.

The Locations and Sets

Despite the huge theme of "outer space," the show would be contained to only a few locations. Ones that are relatable to our audience. There is a very ocean-centric look to Poseidia but without actually being underwater. The dwellings are reminiscent of 1950s homes but with a sea-life twist.

The Blastmaster 1

The Blastmaster 1 is the space shuttle that the Twiggs headed off into outer space in. It was sponsored by Snikky-Snax so there is a massive Snikky-Snax logo on the side. The engine was seriously damaged in the crash-landing, but most of the body work and internal workings are still in place and it functions as the Twigg's home. Even though the Twiggs were offered a Poseidian dwelling, they prefer to live in the Blastmaster, as it reminds them of Earth. Axl is constantly trying to repair it ("only 876 more things to fix and we'll be off!"), so he is usually in the engine room. Its interior could be described as "distressed space age"—a bit like a Vintage Airstream Trailer. All the kids have their own bedrooms, plus there is a communal kitchen/dining area as well as a pole for people to slide down to get from one level to the next.

The Kelp-U-Like

The Kelp-U-Like is the nearest thing Poseidians have to a Diner. It's where everyone gathers for fun and entertainment and any strange Poseidian traditions that need a bit of leg room. It's the home of the "Bell That Is Never Rung" and any number of ancient Poseidian artifacts. Mr. Mussel is usually there to make sure everything runs smoothly and there's no trouble. There is a small stage and the menu is mainly kelp related. Kelp Burger, Kelp in a Basket, Kelp Splits, and, if you're lucky, a Kelpabocker Glory: . . . SO get on down!

The Shoal School

The Shoal School is the school for Poseidian children. The age range is from 200 to 2,000 podyears. Mrs. Gourami is the teacher. Poseidian children of all ages go to the Shoal School to learn how to be good Poseidian citizens. There is a Poseidian equivalent to most Earth subjects; History, Geography, and Math, and so on. Plus, there is a large playing field outside where the pupils can engage in sports. The pupils of the Shoal School can even learn Poseidian, a peculiar guttural language that is rarely spoken any more, mainly because it makes people throw up while they are speaking it.

Kelp! Kelp! Kelp!

There is a local general store where anything you need can be either bought or ordered. It sells food, clothes, and household items and the "appliance creatures" everyone uses to run their homes (which are all displayed in a back room). It's run by Miss Finn, who manages to get most things people need even though it's a mystery how she does it. [Note: there have been sightings of shady characters handing things to her in the dead of night and small parachutes coming down from the sky near her backyard.]

Poseidian Dwellings

In a typical Poseidian dwelling, the building materials are reminiscent of anything you might find under the sea. Rock, coral, and driftwood being the main components, combined with a smattering of space debris. It's open plan with dangly seaweed curtains and sea sponge pillows. Furnishings are usually seashell related.

Recycling is big news on Poseidia so nothing is wasted, and there would also be a "Flintstonian" usage of smaller sealike creatures as household appliances and pets. This will give scope for visual jokes and fill in the gaps where there would usually be the need for something powered by electricity. Examples might include creatures that eat rubbish, one that emits music, one that emits light, and one that has a mouth like a washing machine (some of the more wealthy residents have one of those).

Beyond the Dwellings

As soon as you leave the town of Neptune, you are pretty much in something that looks like a desert, but an alien planet desert. There are mounds and craters, kelp forests, kelp farms, coral swamps, salt streams, and various places that are ripe for exploration and play.

Episodes

The episodes would be character driven and focus on Matt, Molly, and their Poseidian friends, but the grown-ups will always be a big part of the action. Poseidia's tranquil culture is both figuratively and literally alien to the Earthly, streetwise, tech-reliant, dysfunctional Twiggs.

The plots will often involve the Twiggs acclimatizing themselves to their new life on an alien fish planet OR their hapless attempts to "Earth-up" Poseidia whether Poseidia is ready for it or not. There will be new sports to compete in, new music to come to terms with and strange fashion, traditions, and habits to embrace.

When Worlds Collide, . . . Compromise!

The show would have an energetic "kitsch-ness" with license to enjoy and celebrate the "outer space" genre, rather like Futurama. The world of Poseidia will have its own look, creatures, rules, and rituals giving us the opportunity to explore diversity, embracing change, making new friends, compromise, and creativity.

Stories

The Firds

Gem is fed up with the Firds. They fly in crazy shoals over her garden and knock down her carefully laid-out garden ornaments. Gem asks Cosgrove to SHOO them away, which he does. Unfortunately, Welk is watching and reports Cosgrove to the authorities. It seems he has committed a serious Poseidian crime.

"Firds are allowed to go wheresoever they please" quotes Welk.

So, what will happen to Cosgrove? He'll be taken to court and tried under Poseidian law. Fortunately, Matt decides he'll make an excellent defense lawyer but Mr. Mussel is determined to get his first ever successful prosecution.

Puffball

Matt is really excited that there is going to be a Puffball tournament. But then, he finds out that a Puffball is a cheerful little creature that looks like a pufferfish *and* the game is noncompetitive. "What is the point of playing??!!" He complains. "You can't kick the ball and you can't win the game!"

Unfortunately, his attempts to liven up the game result in a very angry Puffball. No one has ever made a Puffball angry before (and people don't like them when they're angry). Watch out, furious Puffball on the rampage!

Father of Invention

Axl has entered the Poseidian Robot Inventing Contest at the Kelp-U-Like and is very confident that he will win. Matt and Molly worry that their dad will fail miserably so they decide to help him. The family build a life-sized Robot with a remote control—which puts Cosgrove's small metal nose out of joint. But all their new Robot seems to do is fall over, but then Matt has an idea. When they get to the contest, he will get inside, . . . which is fine until Dorsal's Robot challenges him to a duel. Only Cosgrove can save the day!

Shell Club

When Molly decides to start Shell Club—a club where everyone collects seashells—everyone is excited. There are badges, a password, and a checklist to tick off all the shells you collect. But there is one type of shell none of them can find—the beautiful Poseidian Conch! Even Miss Finn doesn't know where that can be found! Poseidia is soon a chaotic hive of collecting activity as the search for the Conch takes hold. But when Matt eventually finds one of the rare Conches, he thinks he's going to be famous. Little does he know that Miss Finn will go to extraordinary lengths to get the Conch for her store, . . . and she's got some friends in very low places.

The Bell That Is Never Rung

Molly is excited. She's going to be interviewing Mr. Mussel about the Un-ringing of the "The Bell That Is Never Rung" for the school newspaper. Matt offers to be her photographer, although she suspects that he just wants to try and ring the bell—a grave Poseidian offence—but he manages to land the job anyway.

Molly sits opposite Mr. Mussel at the Kelp-U-Like as he eats a kelp burger and drones on about the history of the bell and how sacred it is to the Poseidians. Matt wants to take a photo of the bell but it is hidden under a sheet until the ceremony. Matt and Molly are getting bored when Mr. Mussel spills Kelpchup on his tie and rushes off to clean it. Matt takes this opportunity to take off the sheet and ring the bell. Molly goes to stop him, there is a struggle, the bell falls on the floor, and cracks. They do their best to make it look like the bell is still under the sheet then they rush out, taking it with them. But will they manage to repair it before the great Un-ringing Ceremony begins?

Space Beans

Axl has bought the shopping back from Kelp! Kelp! Kelp! and in it Matt is fascinated to find a tin of fluorescent beans. There is a knock at the door. Miss Finn bursts in and tells them that they shouldn't eat the beans—they are highly unsuitable for anyone not descended from sea mammals! Too late. They hear a loud burp, and all turn to see Matt, sitting at the table with fluorescent bean stains around his mouth and an empty can in front of him!

Crustacia is really excited! Matt will be ill and she hasn't had a patient for ages! Everyone is very relieved that they have a healer on hand . . . Unfortunately, that healer is Crustacia and Matt is the worst patient on the planet.

FILM AND TV PROGRAM REFERENCES

Films

Aladdin (1992), [Film] Dir. Ron Clements, John Musker, USA: Walt Disney Pictures. USA.

American History (1992), [Film] Dir. Chris Graves, Trey Parker, USA.

An American Tail (1986), [Film] Dir. Don Bluth, USA: Amblin Entertainment, Sullivan Studios.

Arthur Christmas (2011), [Film] Dir. Sarah Smith, Barry Cook, USA/UK: Aardman Features, Sony Pictures Imageworks.

Batman Hush (2019), [Video] Dir. Justin Copeland, USA: Warner Bros. Animation.

Bear Story (2014), [Short Film] Dir. Gabriel Osorio Vargas, Chile: Punkrobot Animation Studio.

Beauty and the Beast (1991), [Film] Dir. Gary Trousdale, Kirk Wise, USA: Walt Disney Pictures, Silver Screen Partners IV.

Bee Movie (2007), [Film] Dir. Steve Hickner, Simon J. Smith, USA: DreamWorks Animation, Columbus 81 Productions.

The Boss Baby (2017), [Film] Dir. Tom McGrath, USA: DreamWorks Animation.

Brave (2012), [Film] Dir. Mark Andrews, Brenda Chapman, USA: Walt Disney Pictures, Pixar Animation Studios.

Cars (2006), [Film] Dir. John Lasseter, USA: Pixar Animation Studios, Walt Disney Pictures.

Chicken Run (2000), [Film] Dir. Peter Lord, Nick Park, UK/USA: Aardman Animations, DreamWorks Animation, Pathe.

Cloudy With a Chance of Meatballs (2009), [Film] Dir. Phil Lord, Christopher Miller, USA: Columbia Pictures, Sony Pictures Animation.

Coco (2017), [Film] Dir. Lee Unkrich, USA: Walt Disney Pictures, Pixar Animation Studios.

The Croods (2013), [Film] Dir. Kirk DeMicco, Chris Sanders, USA: DreamWorks Animation.

Cue Ball Cat—Tom and Jerry (1950), [Short Film] Dir. William Hanna and Joseph Barbera. USA: MGM Cartoon Studio, Loew's.

Curse of the Were-Rabbit (2005), [Film] Dir. Steve Box, Nick Park, UK/USA: Aardman Animations, DreamWorks Animation.

Despicable Me (2010), [Film] Dir. Pierre Coffin, Chris Renaud, USA/France: Universal Pictures, Illumination Entertainment.

Ethel and Ernest (2016), [Film] Dir. Roger Mainwood, UK/Luxembourg: BBC, BFI, Ffilm Cymru Wales.

Fantastic Mr Fox (2009), [Film] Dir. Wes Anderson, USA/UK: Twentieth Century Fox, American Empirical Pictures.

Fast and Furry-ous (1949), [Short Film] Dir. Chuck Jones, USA: Warner Bros.

Father and Daughter (2000), [Short Film] Dir. Michael Dudok de Wit, UK/Belgium/Netherlands: CinéTé Filmproductie BV, Cloudrunner Ltd.

Finding Nemo (2003), [Film] Dir. Andrew Stanton, USA: Pixar Animation Studios, Walt Disney Pictures.

Flushed Away (2006), [Film] Dir. David Bowers, Sam Fell, USA: Aardman Animations, DreamWorks Animation.

Frozen (2013), [Film] Dir. Chris Buck, Jennifer Lee, USA: Walt Disney Animation Studios.

Gnomeo and Juliet (2011), [Film] Dir. Kelly Asbury, UK/USA: Touchstone Pictures, Rocket Pictures.

The Great Escape (1963), [Film] Dir. John Sturges, USA: The Mirisch Company, Alpha Corp.

The Great Mouse Detective (1986), [Film] Dir. Ron Clements, Burny Mattinson, David Michener, John Musker, USA: Walt Disney Pictures, Silver Screen Partners II.

Hair Love (2019), [Short Film] Dir. Matthew A. Cherry, Everett Downing Jr, Bruce W. Smith, USA: Matthew A. Cherry Entertainment, Chasing Miles.

Home Alone (1990), [Film] Dir. Chris Columbus, USA: Hughes Entertainment, Twentieth Century Fox.

Hotel Transylvania (2012), [Film] Dir. Genndy Tartakovsky, USA: Columbia Pictures, Sony Pictures Animation.

Hotel Transylvania 2 (2015), [Film] Dir. Genndy Tartakovsky, USA: Columbia Pictures, LStar Capital, Sony Pictures Animation.

How to Train Your Dragon (2010), [Film] Dir. Dean DeBlois, Chris Sanders, USA: DreamWorks Animation.

The Incredibles (2004), [Film] Dir. Brad Bird, USA: Pixar Animation Studios, Walt Disney Pictures.

Inside Out (2015), [Film] Dir. Pete Docter, USA: Pixar Animation Studios, Walt Disney Pictures.

Joker (2019), [Film] Dir. Todd Phillips, USA: Warner Bros.

The Jungle Book (1967), [Film] Dir. Wolfgang Reitherman, USA: Walt Disney Productions.

Klaus (2019), [Film] Dir. Sergio Pablos, Spain: The SPA Studios, Atresmedia Cine.

Kubo and the Two Strings (2016), [Film] Dir. Travis Knight, USA/Japan: Focus Features, Laika Entertainment.

Kung Fu Panda (2008), [Film] Dir. Mark Osborne, John Stevenson, USA: DreamWorks Animation.

Lady and the Tramp (1955), [Film] Dir. Clyde Geronimi, Wilfred Jackson, Hamilton Luske, USA: Walt Disney Productions.

The Lego Batman Movie (2017), [Film] Dir. Chris McKay, USA/Denmark: DC Entertainment, LEGO System A/S, Lin Pictures.

The Lion King (1994), [Film] Dir. Roger Allers, Rob Minkoff, USA: Walt Disney Pictures.

Look at Life (1965), [Short Film] Dir. George Lucas, USA: University of Southern California.

Love Actually (2003), [Film] Dir. Richard Curtis, USA/UK/France: Working Title Films.

Magnolia (1999), [Film] Dir. Paul Thomas Anderson, USA: Ghoulardi Film Company.

The Meaning of Life (2005), [Short Film] Dir. Don Hertzfeldt, USA: Bitter Films.

Mickey's Once Upon a Christmas (1999), [Video] Dir. Jun Falkenstein, Alex Mann, Bradley Raymond, Toby Shelton, Bill Speers, USA: Disney Television Animation. Walt Disney Feature Animation.

Minions (2015), [Film] Dir. Kyle Balda, Pierre Coffin, USA: Illumination Entertainment.

Missing Link (2019), [Film] Dir. Chris Butler, Canada/USA: Laika Entertainment, Annapurna Pictures, Digital One.

Moana (2016), [Film] Dir. Ron Clements, John Musker, USA: Hurwitz Creative, Walt Disney Animation Studios, Walt Disney Pictures.

The Nightmare Before Christmas (1993), [Film] Dir. Henry Selick, USA, Touchstone Pictures, Skellington Productions Inc.

Oliver and Company (1988), [Film] Dir. George Scribner, USA: Silver Screen Partners III, Walt Disney Pictures.

One Hundred and One Dalmatians (1961), [Film] Dir. Clyde Geronimi, Hamilton Luske, Wolfgang Reitherman, USA: Walt Disney Productions.

ParaNorman (2012), [Film] Dir. Chris Butler, Sam Fell, USA: Laika Entertainment.

Partly Cloudy (2009), [Short Film] Dir. Peter Sohn, USA: Pixar Animation Studios.

Persepolis (2007), [Film] Dir. Vincent Paronnaud, Marjane Satrapi, France/USA: 2.4.7. Films.

Peter Pan (1953), [Film] Dir. Clyde Geronimi, Wilfred Jackson, Hamilton Luske, USA: Walt Disney Productions.

The Present (2014), [Short Film] Dir. Jacob Frey, Germany: Filmakademie Baden-Württemberg.

The Princess and the Frog (2009), [Film] Dir. Ron Clements, John Musker, USA: Walt Disney Pictures.

Pulp Fiction (1994), [Film] Dir. Quentin Tarantino, USA: A Band Apart, Jersey Films.

Puss in Boots (2011), [Film] Dir. Chris Miller, USA: DreamWorks Animation.

Rango (2011), [Film] Dir. Gore Verbinski, USA: Blind Wink Productions, GK Films.

Ratatouille (2007), [Film] Dir. Brad Bird, USA: Walt Disney Pictures, Pixar Animation Studios.

Robin Hood (1973), [Film] Dir. Wolfgang Reitherman, USA: Walt Disney Productions.

Sausage Party (2016), [Film] Dir. Greg Tiernan, Conrad Vernon, USA/Canada: Annapurna Pictures, Columbia Pictures, Point Grey Pictures, Nitrogen Studios Canada.

Shrek (2001), [Film] Dir. Andrew Adamson, Vicky Jenson, USA: DreamWorks Animation, Pacific Data Images (PDI).

Shrek the Third (2007), [Film] Dir. Chris Miller, USA: DreamWorks Animation, Pacific Data Images (PDI).

Sing (2016), [Film] Dir. Garth Jennings, Japan/USA: Dentsu, Fuji Television Network, Illumination Entertainment, Universal Pictures.

Sleeping Beauty (1959), [Film] Dir. Clyde Geronimi, USA: Walt Disney Animation Studios, Walt Disney Productions.

Snow White and the Seven Dwarfs (1937), [Film] Dir. David Hand, USA: Walt Disney Productions.

Tangled (2010), [Film] Dir. Nathan Greno, Byron Howard, USA: Walt Disney Pictures.

Toy Story (1995), [Film] Dir. John Lasseter, USA: Pixar Animation Studios, Walt Disney Pictures.

Toy Story 3 (2010), [Film] Dir. Lee Unkrich, USA: Walt Disney Pictures, Pixar Animation Studios.

Toy Story 4 (2019), [Film] Dir. Josh Cooley, USA: Walt Disney Pictures, Pixar Animation Studios.

Up (2009), [Film] Dir. Pete Docter, USA: Pixar Animation Studios, Walt Disney Pictures.

Wallace and Gromit: A Close Shave (1995), [Short] Dir. Nick Park, UK: Aardman Animations, BBC Bristol.

Zootopia (2016), Dir. Byron Howard, Rich Moore, USA: Walt Disney Pictures.

TV Shows

8 Simple Rules… for Dating My Teenage Daughter (2002), [TV program] ABC, September 17.

The Adventures of Paddington (2020), [TV program] Nickelodeon, Nick Jnr, January 20.

Adventure Time (2010), [TV program] Cartoon Network, April 5.

Batman: The Animated Series (1992), [TV program] Fox Kids, September 5.

The Big Bang Theory (2006), [TV program] CBS, May 1.

Black-ish (2014), [TV program] ABC, September 24.

Bob's Burgers (2011), [TV program] Fox, January 9.
Bob's Burgers, Sexy Dance Healing (2016), [TV program] Fox, February 21.
Breaking Bad (2008), [TV program] AMC, January 20.
The Bugs Bunny Show (1960), [TV program] ABC, October 11.
The Charlie Brown and Snoopy Show (1983), [TV program] CBS, September 17.
Curious George (2006), [TV program] PBS Kids, September 4.
The Deep (2015), [TV program] Family Chrgd, December 1.
Desperate Housewives (2004), [TV program] ABC, October 3.
Dinotrux (2015), [TV program] Netflix, August 14.
Doc McStuffins (2012), [TV program] Disney Junior, March 23.
Dora the Explorer (2000), [TV program] Nickelodeon, August 14.
Downton Abbey (2010), [TV program] ITV, September 26.
Everybody Loves Raymond (1996), [TV program] CBS, September 13.
Family Guy (1999), [TV program] Fox, January 31.
Family Guy, Absolutely Babulous (2019), [TV program] Fox, October 13.
Family Guy, Blue Harvest (2007), [TV program] Fox, September 23.
Family Guy, Love, Blactually (2008), [TV program] Fox, September 28.
Fawlty Towers (1975), [TV program] BBC Two, September 19.
The Flintstones (1960), [TV program] ABC, May 1.
Friends (1994), [TV program] NBC, September 22 .
Frasier (1993), [TV program] NBC, September 16.
Fresh Off the Boat (2015), [TV program] ABC, February 4.
Futurama (1999), [TV program] Fox, March 28.
Hong Kong Phooey (1974), [TV program] ABC, September 7.
Jake and the Never Land Pirates (2011), [TV program] Disney Junior, February 14.
King of the Hill (1997), [TV program] Fox, January 12.
Leave it to Beaver (1957), [TV Program] CBS, April 23.
Lego Marvel Superheroes: Maximum Overload (2013), [TV program] Netflix, November 5.
The Mandalorian (2019), [TV Program] Disney+, November 12.
The Middle (2009), [TV program] ABC, September 30.
Modern Family (2009), [TV program] ABC, September 23.
Paw Patrol (2013), [TV program] TVOKids, August 27.
Paw Patrol, Pups Go for the Gold, (2018) [TV program] Nickelodeon, March 8.
Peppa Pig (2004), [TV program] Channel 5, May 31.
The Phil Silvers Show (1955), [TV program] CBS, September 20.
Rick and Morty (2013), [TV program] Adult Swim, December 2.
The Road Runner Show (1966), [TV program] CBS, September 10.
Salem's Lot (1979), [TV program] CBS, November 17.
Scooby Doo, Where Are You! (1969), [TV program] CBS, September 13.
Schitt's Creek (2015), [TV Program] CBC, January 13.
Scrubs (2001), [TV program] NBC, October 2.

Seinfeld (1989), [TV program] NBC, July 5.
Sense8 (2015), [TV program] Netflix, June 5.
Shameless (2004), [TV program] Channel 4, January 13.
Shark Tank (2009), [TV program] ABC, August 9.
The Simpsons (1989), [TV program] Fox, December 17.
The Simpsons Treehouse of Horror (1990), [TV program] Fox, October 25.
South Park (1997), [TV program] Comedy Central, August 13.
Timmy Time (2009), [TV program] BBC, April 6.
Tom and Jerry (1940), [TV program] MGM, February 10.
Top Cat (1961), [TV program] ABC, September 27.
Two and a Half Men (2003), [TV program] CBS, September 22.
Wacky Races (1968), [TV program] CBS, September 14.
Watership Down (2018), [TV program] BBC, December 22.
We Bare Bears (2015), [TV program] Cartoon Network, July 27.
The X Factor (2004), [TV program] ITV, September 4.

THINKY TIME GUIDE

1. Creating a fantasy show idea.
2. Looking at hyper-reality.
3. Why animation?
4. Why is the goal important to the character?
5. Identifying obstacles.
6. Plotlines: A plots and B plots.
7. How to plot the second act.
8. Three-act structure.
9. Plotting the emotional goal.
10. Character archetypes.
11. Creating a character.
12. Adjusting the drop.
13. Metaphorical family relationships.
14. Creating short film concepts.

Dialogue Workshops Are in Chapter 19

1. Getting down the basics.
2. Character motivation.
3. Voice and attitude.
4. Keeping it visual, increasing the action.
5. Making it brief.

Case Study Guide

Central Character: *Family Guy "Absolutely Babulous"*
Three-Act Structure: *Zootopia*
Three-Act Structure: *Paw Patrol "Pups Go for The Gold"*
Emotional Goal: *Shrek*
Writing for an Existing Show: *Bob's Burgers*
Short Film: *The Meaning of Life*
Breaking the Format: *Frozen*
Breaking the Format: *Toy Story 3*

INDEX

www.ingramcontent.com/pod-product-compliance
Ingram Content Group UK Ltd.
Pitfield, Milton Keynes, MK11 3LW, UK
UKHW031251020325
455690UK00007B/98